OPEN,

M000015069

"*Open, Honest, and Direct* is not just a book, it's a way of leading your people by creating a culture of transparency, vulnerability, and courage. I love how Aaron weaves in the science behind each key leadership skill through stories and actionable advice. The book is not only insightful, but it's also practical. It gives you the tools to apply with your team today. A must-read for any entrepreneur."

—Craig Wortmann, Clinical Professor of Innovation and Entrepreneurship at
Northwestern University's Kellogg School of Management

"Unlike most business books that focus on what a leader needs to know rather than what a leader needs to do, *Open, Honest, and Direct* provides an easy-to-follow roadmap to develop four fundamental skills that will allow powerful leaders to unlock people's potential and get the most out of their teams."

—Sam Yagan, co-founder of SparkNotes and OkCupid,
former CEO of Match Group, CEO of ShopRunner, and
one of TIME Magazine's 100 Most Influential People in the World

"One responsibility of today's organizations is to help the individuals in the company grow and fulfill their potential and goals, and the individual's responsibility is to have the courage to take advantage of and action on the opportunities the organization presents—it's what builds a strong culture. Not only does this book touch on the key topics of organizational responsibility, leadership, and human behavior—it also provides readers with real tools and actionable items to put in place with their teams."

—Peter Rahal, co-founder of RXBAR

"A book on leadership is worth so much more when the ideas within it become actionable. Aaron captures the simple, human essence of leadership with practical steps to make it a conscious daily practice."

—David Mead, co-author of *Find Your Why* with Simon Sinek
and Peter Docker and Igniter at Simon Sinek, Inc.

AARON LEVY

OPEN, HONEST, & DIRECT

A GUIDE TO UNLOCKING YOUR TEAM'S POTENTIAL

RIVER GROVE
BOOKS

Published by River Grove Books
Austin, TX
www.rivergrovebooks.com

Distributed by River Grove Books

Design and composition by Greenleaf Book Group
Cover design by Greenleaf Book Group

Publisher's Cataloging-in-Publication data is available.

Paperback ISBN: 978-1-63299-237-6

Hardcover ISBN: 978-1-63299-239-0

eBook ISBN: 978-1-63299-238-3

First Edition

This book is dedicated to my wife, business partner, and best friend, Kim. None of this would be possible without her energy, passion, and critical eye.

CONTENTS

ATTRACT AND RETAIN TOP TALENT

Think of the last time you tried to roll out a new process to your team. You delivered a clean presentation that was simple and easy to digest. You gave your team time to ask questions and gain clarity. You even followed up with an email recapping what was expected of them. You did everything you could to provide the knowledge, believing it would lead to a smooth and intuitive rollout.

But why, only a few days later, are only a *handful* of people following the new process? Generating a change in the behavior of your people requires more than just telling them what to do and how to do it; it requires them to take action. It's the same reason only 20% of people ever accomplish their New Year's resolutions.[1] Why, when people know better, do they not *do* better? It's not that people don't know what to do; the problem is that they don't take action.

We tend to believe knowledge leads directly to action; that is, someone knows what to do, then they do it. I find this to be a fallacy in our understanding of human behavior—and the reasons for this are fascinating.

WHY WE DO WHAT WE DO

To better understand the knowledge-to-action gap, I took a deep dive into the science of human behavior some years ago. I wanted to find out why people do what they do and what triggers some people to take action in their lives while others do not. I looked back to the history of *Homo sapiens*, trying to understand where our instincts originated. I read philosophy to better appreciate the perspective on the human condition from generations past. I researched the perplexities of the human brain and cognitive biases from behavioral economists like Daniel Kahneman and Amos Tversky and looked at the importance of intrinsic motivation in driving human behavior from the likes of Ed Deci and Richard Ryan. I explored how social constructs nudge our decision making in one direction or another. And I even looked at casinos and grocery stores to understand how space design—the environment you're surrounded by—can influence your decisions.

All of this research helped paint a picture of why we do what we do. But it wasn't enough. I really wanted to know how this worked in real life, with real people. I was fortunate to be the first employee at a health and well-being coaching and education organization right out of college, led by two physicians who viewed medicine from a whole new perspective. Instead of seeking to fix the sick, they wanted to see how we could look upstream at the problem; they dove into the question of human behavior with the very same curiosity I had. As the director of education and delivery at that organization, I had the perfect opportunity to test out these theories in real life.

Our client base gave me the chance to work with thousands of leaders from all over the country, across varied socioeconomic backgrounds, generations, and denominations. It became my playground to explore behavior change. I started testing what worked to trigger change in people's lives—from yearlong coaching, weeklong training programs, and experiential workshops to lunch-and-learns, webinars, and even animated videos.

We tried everything, and through these mini experiments, I discovered two key insights that made a profound impact on my future, ultimately leading me here.

Discovery 1

I found what really works to drive a human being from knowledge to action and how to do this rapidly and effectively. All of the work I've done with leaders since has been based on this key learning and even informs how I've laid out this book for you to read. I care more about you taking action as a result of reading this book than anything else, so the book is designed in a way for you to *do*, not to simply *know*.

Discovery 2

In my work with thousands of leaders, I noticed what gives me the most joy is seeing the light switch go on for a leader. And once the light turns on, I'm awed at the way these leaders quickly take action, not just in that one area but also across various other domains in their lives and business. I uncovered how far-reaching and profound one intentional, consistent change can be on a leader and a company's performance.

The feeling of helping someone tap into their potential invigorates me, and even now, writing about it, I feel my heart beating faster with energy and excitement. This clarity shifted my perspective of the world and my role within it. I realized that helping people unlock their potential is what I love doing. It's what fills me up. And my eyes immediately opened to the problems and possibilities around me. I began asking some different questions of myself.

How can I serve more people in unlocking their potential? Where could I maximize my impact? What problem would I be solving? In searching for a better answer to these questions, I was led to a $30 billion problem and realized I could do something about it.

MILLENNIAL TURNOVER: THE $30 BILLION PROBLEM

For quite some time, I've observed people—millennials in particular—jumping from job to job, sometimes leaving incredible positions for reasons I couldn't logically understand. I had a friend, Harry, who was making well over $150,000 at twenty-five years old. He kept getting promotions and raises at a rapidly growing company, where he worked with a few of his good friends—and they even had a barista on staff. Yet only three months after his most recent promotion, Harry quit.

The crazy part is that he wasn't recruited by another company; he wasn't starting his own business. He simply left to sit on his couch and figure things out. I remember being really confused. He seemed to have all the things you'd want at a company, and yet he still left. I asked him what his reasons were at the time, and he told me, "I didn't feel like I had the opportunity to grow and develop myself, and if I couldn't see myself there in five years, why should I stay?"

Harry's story sparked a fire in me. I began interviewing friends, clients, and anyone who would talk to me about their job and their future desires. Virtually all of them said they were in the process of searching for a new job or not planning to stay with their organization for more than two or three years. After more research, I found these stories weren't all that unique. Millennials everywhere—even today—are going from job to job, staying months instead of years. According to a recent survey, only 27% of millennials were expected to stay at their current company for the next four years.[2]

As a millennial myself, I wanted to know what was going on. What was causing this enormous turnover?

What I found was simple yet powerful. In almost every leave story, I observed a perceived lack of one or more of these factors, factors that apply to your workforce today:

1. The desire to do work that makes an impact

2. The need to feel connected to your team, company, and boss

3. The belief that your company cares deeply about your
    growth and development

Millennials want to do work that makes an impact, to do something with real purpose to it. This doesn't necessarily mean working for a nonprofit whose mission is to rid the world of illness or poverty. Millennials want to know, within whatever company or organization they join, that the work they do matters and how it plays a role in the company's success.

I consistently see how a millennial's desire to be heard and recognized is often misconstrued as a desire for instant gratification or to be coddled. In reality, their behavior has to do with a desire for a feeling of connectedness to their company and the feeling that their opinions and perspectives are valued by their leaders and team.

Like Harry, millennials' most common reason for leaving a job is that they don't feel their company truly cares about their growth and development. Often, it breaks down at the manager level, with the manager seeing the millennial as a to-do on their weekly task list instead of as a future leader to grow and nurture.

You might be thinking these are not just millennial needs; these are basic human needs any person wants in life. Don't we all want to make a difference, to be heard, and to grow and develop?

You're right. These needs are not unique to millennials—although there is a key difference. Millennials not only need these factors in their life but also have come to expect them from their workplace, which is vastly different from the Gen Xers, baby boomers, and traditionalists who came before them.

To better explain, there are a variety of reasons—including the changing world of work, the nature of our current on-demand society, and various inciting incidents—that have affected the experiences of an entire generation. (The generations conversation is a different conversation for another day. If you want to know more about why the millennial generation is different, I share more in the bonus chapter at the end of the book.) What I noticed from all of this was a group of people who were not satisfied with their work, who were not unlocking their potential, and who were hoping that the next role they landed would magically tap into it. It was a disturbing hope.

I was lucky; I found my potential in my very first role. Many others aren't so lucky.

I looked at the problem from the perspective of an organization or a business leader and found that employee turnover costs US businesses more than $30 billion per year. And it's not a problem that can simply be avoided by not hiring millennials.[3]

According to a 2016 Gallup Study, millennials already account for 38% of the entire workforce and are expected to be 75% of the workforce by 2025.[4] Rather than being an issue about millennials, this is an issue about the largest population in the workforce—one critical to the growth and future success of any business.

It's a two-sided problem, one where the employee wants to be at their best, to reach their potential, but has no idea of where to do this, how it happens, and what to do to ensure their next job is the one that connects them with their potential. The other side of the problem comes from companies wanting their employees to be at their best and not knowing how to get the most out of their people. Both sides are losing, and an end doesn't seem to be in sight. One reason is that it's even easier now more than ever for employees to leave when something's not working because the labor market is so competitive. The shorter employee life cycle only makes this problem harder and more critical to solve.

THE WAR FOR TALENT IS REAL

Record low unemployment is making it harder and harder for growing companies to find and hire top talent and, conversely, easier for talent to switch jobs. I was at lunch a few months ago with four successful entrepreneurs, and like most conversations, the topic quickly turned to their most pressing concern—hiring talent. One founder rolled his eyes, another sighed, and they all complained about the difficulty and the fierce competition around attracting top talent. These entrepreneurs are impressive; one just raised $40 million, another is on Crain's Fastest Growing Companies, and they were all exasperated with the struggle to find the right employees to grow their companies.

Although low unemployment is good for the economy, the lower the unemployment rate is, the harder it is for businesses to find good employees. According to the Bureau of Labor Statistics, the unemployment rate dropped to 3.9%, which is the lowest point since the late 1960s. If you take a deeper dive into the data over time, you'll find unemployment for adults over twenty-five is 3.1%, and for those with a bachelor's degree or higher, it's at 2%—making it even harder to find talent with a degree.[5]

The issue of attracting talent is real. Attracting talent is something companies must focus their energy and resources on. Yet, in meeting with 400+ businesses in the past twenty-four months, I've noticed a trend—more of a trap—that most of these companies fall into.

Companies look at the problem of attracting top talent, and, instead of taking a long-term approach, they often focus on a short-term solution: throwing money at it. It's as if they are dealing with a leaking bucket, and, instead of taking time to fix the leak, they just keep adding more water to replace what's flowing out.

As people continue to leave, companies try to solve the problem by adding more people to replace them. They focus on filling the bucket with more talent and making the opening of the bucket look prettier so more people will want to jump in.

A perfect example of this can be seen in a fast-growing tech company in Chicago—let's call them Company X—that just raised $7 million. Most of the funding is going into hiring tech talent to develop Company X's product for new markets and into building out its gorgeous new office space with a game room, nap room, kombucha on tap, and a cereal bar. To hire the needed developers, coders, and digital marketers, the company pays a recruiting firm 25% of each new hire's starting salary. At an average salary of $150,000, Company X pays out $750,000 across three recruitment companies just to hire twenty new employees. At the company's current turnover rate of 30%, Company X will also need to hire six *more* people in the next year just to maintain its team; it's throwing away $225,000 to recruiters each year.

Most companies hire recruiters, pay exorbitant recruitment fees, enhance their perk packages, and continue to raise salaries—even though people are leaving almost as fast as they are hired. The cyclical nature of this problem, which most companies find themselves in, creates a huge opportunity—one that only a few organizations have tapped into. Instead of focusing on the trap of attracting talent—on filling the bucket with more water—strategic leaders take the time to fix the hole in the bucket by focusing on talent retention.

FIXING THE LEAK

This is where I've decided to put my energy. It's how I've found I can best help people unlock their potential. You may have heard the phrase, "It's cheaper to keep a client than to find a new one." I believe the same holds true for your employees. I've seen how companies who provide deep-rooted intrinsic value for their employees win in the long term.

I'm talking about creating an environment where people want to come to work, where they can see the perceptible impact their daily actions have on the business, and where they can grow their skills, leaving better than when they first walked through your doors. It's about creating a culture that is open, honest, and direct.

If you don't believe this is possible, take a look at Hireology, a frequent name on various lists of the best places to work and one of the Inc.'s fastest growing companies. I've had a chance to take a close look at the structure and leadership of Hireology. They have a culture of people who love to work for them, and they reap the rewards of resources spent on developing their people rather than on solely attracting new people. Hireology and companies like it provide autonomy (the freedom for employees to do their work), competency (the opportunity for employees to succeed and develop mastery in a specific area), and connection (an environment where employees feel connected to each other and see the impact of their work). These factors match the needs of humans as defined by Ed Deci and Richard Ryan's self-determination theory of human motivation.[6] Hireology is a great example of a company with clear values, vision, and mission; that ensures its managers are leaders, not doers; and that provides a structured operating system for its employees to grow within.

MOST MANAGERS SUCK

Creating an environment of intrinsic motivation for your employees is much easier said than done. To make it happen, your managers need to be powerful leaders. An employee's need for impact, connection, and growth in the workplace are all perceptions. Even if you provide great resources for your employees, it doesn't guarantee they'll see them as resources.

One of my good friends, Ty, was working at a fast-growing company that provided unlimited funds for his personal development. He could buy books on Amazon, sign up for courses to take online, or go to conferences to better himself. And yet, he still quit. Why? He quit three months after his boss left for a different company, and, as he shared with me, "My last boss was awesome. I loved working with her, and I learned so much in such a short time. My new boss doesn't really care about me or my growth, so why stay and do the work when I can go learn more on my own?"

As a business leader, this can be baffling, knowing you are investing in your people and not having them recognize it. It's because the biggest influence on an employee's perception of her company and her place within the company is her manager.

When a business leader needs to fill a management role, the natural thought is to look at top performers. We pluck them out of their role as individual contributors and put them into a management role, as a team lead. We do this because they are good at their job, not because they are good at leading people. This is the problem. A top performer will not necessarily be a great leader. Leading and performing require vastly different skill sets. In fact, fewer than 10% of employees naturally have the tools and skills to be great leaders.[7] We often pick the wrong person because we are not looking at the right set of skills. We look at their key performance indicators, not their ability to listen to others or deliver critical feedback. We fail to assess their people skills, ultimately setting them up for failure.

FINDING YOUR COMPETITIVE ADVANTAGE

I work with companies to fix the leak in their bucket by empowering managers with the tools, skills, and training to be better leaders of people. When you focus on empowering your managers to be coaches rather than micromanagers and on adding value to the talent you already have, you will get employees who want to stay and give you their all. Talent will find you because they want to be a part of what's going on at your company. Employees will be engaged; they'll give their extra discretionary effort to their work instead of to their Instagram account or side hustle because their managers help them see their impact, because they'll feel connected to the company, and because they'll experience constant growth, regardless of title changes or promotions. Managers will be leaders and not simply doers because they will have the tools and skills needed to lead.

When this happens—when you have a company of open, honest, and direct leaders, a group of leaders and not simply doers, of coaches and not simply managers—you'll be in rare company. Most organizations don't take the time to be so thoughtful, deliberate, and focused on developing the skills of their leaders. You'll unlock the potential of your organization, and your people will become your competitive advantage.

That's the opportunity I'm so excited to share with you and why I'm writing this book.

HOW TO USE THIS BOOK

This book is designed to share knowledge from my work with thousands of leaders and to provide you with the practical tools and skills to apply to your leadership and with your team, whether your needs are for an entire global organization, a growing team, or just a department of one. In sharing these lessons, tools, and skills, I hope you can learn from my mistakes and experiences to more rapidly develop your team of open, honest, and direct leaders. To do this, I've broken the book up into three parts.

Part 1

Part 1 is about how you can make sure to get it right when hiring and promoting managers in your company or team. As leaders, we tend to skip this step and go straight into how you make your managers better. I advise you not to skip this part of the book, as it can save you a lot of pain later on in the development of your leaders.

Part 2

The tools in part 2 get much more tactical; I'll share activities, check-lists, and frameworks to serve as a practical guide to developing the four key skills to make you and your team more powerful leaders.

Part 3

Finally, we'll bring it all together, walking you through the steps to get started today with plans to organize and schedule your leader-ship successfully and without too much headache!

The goal of this book is for you to be able to put, if nothing else, at least one new skill into practice in your life as a leader. If out of all the insights shared and gained, you put one idea into consistent action, you'll have succeeded. Small changes taken consistently over time lead to profound impact.

Enjoy the read. I can't wait to hear what action you've put in place on the other side of this book. Many of the frameworks, models, and checklists featured in the book are also available on *openhonestanddirect.com* for your use. That's where you can con-nect with me directly to find out more about an idea in this book, ask a question, or share a win. Please do connect. I want to hear from you; it's what fills me up!

Note

For some of the stories in this book, I share the challenges clients and friends discussed with me. As a means to respect their confidentiality, I've changed their names.

For other stories, I've kept the names of clients (with their permission, of course!) and provided more specifics about their situation to give you more context and relatability to a situation you may be facing.

PART 1

CHOOSE THE RIGHT MANAGERS

It is crucial that you choose the right people as the foundation of your company's leadership. To secure that foundation, we need to know why managers fail, how good ones succeed, and how to help encourage that success in your team. Without all three pieces, your leadership team will fail.

For instance, what happens if you have good managers who aren't given the time or tools to connect with, evaluate, and support their reports? You get a disconnected team. You get frustrated managers and employees. You get a revolving door of talent. But with top-down support—leading by example—you can give your managers every chance to help their team grow and succeed.

In part 1, you'll find key checklists to follow when looking for the right manager (chapter 1), an understanding of the key skills all great leaders possess (chapter 2), a deeper explanation of how habit formation works (chapter 3), and a framework to more rapidly change behaviors within your company today.

Let's start putting the pieces together.

Chapter 1

WHY MOST MANAGERS SUCK

*"I most seriously believe that one does people the best service
by giving them some elevating work to do and thus
indirectly elevating them."*

—Albert Einstein

Intention: It's on you to set your managers up for success.

Let's face it: Most managers suck. We will first take a focused look upstream at this problem and explore three key questions for hiring and promoting the right manager for your team. Choosing the right manager can make or break the success of your team and company, so it's critical to get this step right. You may not feel as though you have the tools or the time to properly vet a manager yourself. We'll discuss ways to give you more clarity throughout the process, making it easier to determine the right hire or promotion and saving you hours and hours of rehiring later on.

WHY TOP PERFORMERS DON'T MAKE GREAT LEADERS

Top performers are promoted into management roles because of their ability to do work well, not because of their ability to lead. The problem with turning your top performers into managers is that their skills as individual contributors don't always directly translate into leadership skills. The skills required to lead are vastly different from the skills required to be a top performer.

Too often, I see organizations promote top performers and then leave them alone to figure out how to run a team. Once they are promoted, top performers-turned-managers typically tend to power through, sticking with what got them there and relying on talents that may not apply well to their new situation. However, what got your manager there—being good at *doing* a job—doesn't necessarily mean they know how to *lead* others doing that job. When they continue to do all the work individually, they turn into what I'd refer to as a super doer rather than a leader, and the negative impact on the team and its success is immediate and profound. Without the right tools and skills, the transition from top performer to manager leads to an inevitable drop in employee performance, increased company turnover, and a lot of frustration for all parties.

This recently happened to one of my clients, Katya. Katya was the corporate hero. She'd mastered the science of success, of getting work done, and had achieved a level of excellence that most others don't reach. After being promoted to partner in her company, she found herself stressed out, overworked, and unsure of how she could keep up as her responsibilities and team grew.

Katya, like most other super doers, fell back on her work ethic. As her company grew, she had trouble saying no to all the various requests coming her way. From client fires to employee questions, Katya found herself increasingly more frazzled. Instead of benefiting from additional team members, she took on more tasks and responsibilities. To ensure success, she double-checked all client emails, orders placed, and proposals sent out. In reviewing every detail, it seemed she hoped her team would learn how to do great work simply by osmosis.

For Katya, things reached a breaking point when she was faced with a several-thousand-dollar mistake one of her employees made for the second time in three weeks. The first time it happened, she blamed the employee. But the second time, Katya realized it wasn't the employee's fault; it was hers.

THE IMPACT OF A BAD MANAGER

Having the wrong person in the wrong seat hurts the business on many levels. Not only is the manager being asked to be accountable for the growth, development, and success of a team of people, but she is also expected to continue performing on the same level herself. The results are often a failure on both ends.

First, you lose a top performer. They go from delivering great work to now having to manage their time between doing the work, leading others, and putting out fires. Instead of doing one thing well, they are now doing many things poorly.

Second, you create a team of frustrated employees who are also not performing. They are frustrated because their manager doesn't support their growth, doesn't communicate clearly, or doesn't help them be better at their work. The frustration can only last so long before you start to lose employees. And it all stems from this single manager promotion.

ACTIVITY: THREE QUESTIONS FOR HIRING RIGHT

- ☐ Does she want to lead?
- ☐ Do I have the right metrics in place to measure her success?
- ☐ Does she have the skills to lead others?

HOW CAN I GET IT RIGHT?

The manager is still the number-one reason people leave their jobs. The impact of picking a bad manager never seems to end for a company. That's why it's so critical to get this right.

The most important thing to do is make sure you have the right people in the right seats. This means taking a step back and looking at your hiring and promotion practices. Before hiring a manager, I recommend first asking yourself these three questions:

Do they want to lead?

The desire to lead is the single biggest factor in the development of a leader. I once had an executive ask me if I thought certain people just aren't meant to lead. Although there are people who seem naturally and intuitively inclined to lead, I've found that anyone can lead if they have the desire to learn and are willing to do the work. I've learned through my work with leaders that those who are the most successful in our training are the people who want it—who want to grow and develop themselves as leaders.

If someone doesn't want to lead, then they shouldn't be doing it, and that's OK too. Sometimes this requires letting go of old mindsets and work structures where managing people is the only way to get ahead in business. It's time to recognize there are other paths to growth within an organization. It's OK to promote individual contributors up the ranks of your organization without giving them a team to lead.

> **Tip:** It can be hard for an individual to recognize that they would rather be a contributor than a leader. Instead of asking them if they want to lead, ask them what excites them about leading a team. Their answer—the way they either light up when talking about others or skip over the team aspect—will give you a better insight into their true desires.

Why do we have to pluck a top individual contributor out of what they are good at and force them into something they don't want to do? There's no reason for it. We can stop this now by promoting those who want to lead into leadership roles while creating other avenues of growth for those who don't. Knowing who wants to lead and who doesn't also enables a company to prevent problems further down the line when it realizes it may not have the right person in the right position.

ACTIVITY: IDENTIFY YOUR INDIVIDUAL CONTRIBUTORS

1. Create a list of all your people managers.
2. Go through each manager on the list one by one and ask yourself:
   a. Does she truly want to lead? (yes, no)
   b. What is the impact of her managing people on your team? (positive, neutral, negative)
   c. Is she better served as an individual contributor? (yes, no)
3. Put a big star by each manager who is a better fit as an individual contributor.
4. Determine your course of action with each manager.

Now that you've identified your people managers who would likely be better off as individual contributors, it's time to determine your course of action. The impact of doing nothing is likely far worse than you might imagine in the moment. Just because someone isn't a fit right now to manage others doesn't mean they have to be demoted or fired. That's counterintuitive if they're great contributors.

EVALUATING MANAGERS				
Manager name	Do they truly want to lead? (yes, no)	What's the impact of their managing people? (positive, neutral, negative)	Are they better served as an individual contributor? (yes, no)	Action to take
Noel	Yes	Neutral	No	Invest in her development as a leader.
Steve	No	Negative	Yes	Share insights with Steve and opportunity to transition to more strategic role where he doesn't manage people.
Latoya	Yes	Positive	Yes	Check in with her to learn what she's doing well and how you can continue to support her.

Often, the most effective transitions have no impact on a person's title, pay, or position in the organizational chart. Rather, the change that's needed will free your leader up from the responsibilities of managing others and give them time to crush it for your organization, thereby performing even more effectively. By keeping certain leaders on as individual contributors and allowing them to continue to thrive within the organization, you create a path others can see for success, one in which career growth is not dependent on managing people.

Do you have the right metrics in place?

Once you've confirmed the answer to the first question and have determined your potential new hire or promotion does want to lead a team, it's time to take an internal look at your metrics. Do you have the priorities and performance metrics aligned for your managers to be successful?

Priorities and performance metrics are the success measures and evaluation milestones for the position. They are what allow both you and your managers to understand what success looks like for them in this role. By understanding these metrics, you can better share them up front with each manager, giving them clarity about their role and your expectations.

Prioritizing your leadership

During a recent check-in meeting, my client asked how it was going with her team. In full transparency, I shared how they have the skills but they don't have the time.

This is something I see frequently from organizations experiencing hypergrowth. As the leader of your organization, you have a picture of what you want the company to be—a beautiful vision of people who love to work for you, who love their coworkers, and who come to work excited to work alongside their boss and team. The only problem is the execution of this vision; that's where most of us fail. We fail because although we *say* it's critical for our leaders to spend time coaching and growing their team, what we *do* conveys the opposite message. Although she wanted her team to develop their skills and although she invested money to do it, my client wasn't showing up as an example they could follow and didn't give them the space needed to actually develop their skills.

People do what you do, not what you say. As the leader of the organization, you are the archetype of what success looks like; you are the corporate hero for your team. If you are constantly running from meeting to meeting, showing up late, pushing meetings over and over again, and generally too busy to spend time developing your leaders, you are sending a specific message and creating a picture of what it takes to succeed in your organization. This CEO was sending a message that getting work done was more important than developing skills to lead more effectively and efficiently, so her leaders didn't do the work it took to develop their leadership toolkit.

One of my clients recently admitted to me that he doesn't do one-on-ones with his executive team. He says it's because he trusts them to do their work and wants to give them autonomy. But autonomy without accountability doesn't work. It's a basic human need to have at least some level of certainty, and people crave structure and accountability, even if they say they don't.

In reading between the lines, it became clear to me that, between board meetings, strategy sessions, and travel, my client had to choose where he spent his hours in the day, and making the time to meet with each person on a biweekly basis was not high enough on the priority list in an already busy schedule. What kind of example does this set for his executive team? By not making time for his team, his leaders then didn't prioritize one-on-one meetings with their own direct reports, and the pattern followed, on and on, down the line, resulting in a company culture that lacked structure and account-ability. And when this happens, people pay for it.

If you want others to lead, you need to prioritize leading your-self, or put someone else in place to lead so you can contribute to the company in other ways. What this looks like is taking the time to have one-on-ones with your people, making sure you check in periodically, and asking your team how you can help serve them. It also means letting your team make mistakes so they can learn from them instead of having you jump in as the savior to fix their errors at the eleventh hour.

Establishing the right performance metrics

It takes time to lead. Depending on how many people you have reporting to you, managing people should take between 20% and 30% of your time. That's at least one day a week, whether you plan it or not. If you don't plan ahead, you'll end up losing that time and more. If you are unable to effectively lead, your reports are left to fend for themselves, which brings about fires. You'll have to stop what you are doing to jump in and help or fix a situation that could have likely been prevented. If you plan ahead and are strategic in your approach, you can get ahead of those major fires.

Does your organization incentivize new leaders to spend time with their direct reports? Or do leaders only get recognized (or paid) when they deliver work? It's crucial to get your performance metrics and incentive structure aligned properly.

Even if your newly hired manager wants to lead others, if they are expected to do the same amount of work or even more while also managing a team of people, something's going to give. Where do you think they'll decide to prioritize their time? On what their bonus compensation is tied to? Or with their team? The answer is obvious: They'll focus on what helps them get their full bonus, not on their team. What gets measured matters.

Tip: Including one or two measures of team performance in your leader's individual performance metrics is a surefire way to make sure you align priorities.

A great example of this comes from Frank Riordan, the president of DMC, a rapidly growing engineering consultancy with offices all across the country. Frank has a wonderful dashboard he uses to assess each of his employee's performance. He looks at three elements: billable hours, projects proposed, and project dollars managed. Each element is scaled as if the employee were only performing one of them, and then a composite score is created to get a weekly snapshot of performance. Frank knows each element is critical to the success of his organization; he recognizes the importance of intentionally taking time to lead and manage his team, and so he assesses his team accordingly.

> **Tip:** Avoid putting more than eight people under one manager. I've found that any number larger than this is simply too many people for one manager to be able to handle well.

It's imperative to set up success measures for your managers. The happiness and well-being of people in your company—and, ultimately, the performance of your company—are tied to the ability of your managers to connect effectively with their direct reports. When you sit down to assess your leaders at the end of the quarter or year, one element of their performance should measure how well their team is performing and how well they lead.

By including performance metrics around people management, your leaders will be able to clearly see where your priorities lie and will motivate them to spend more time focused on developing the skills it takes to be a great leader.

Do they have the skills to lead others?

This might seem to be the first question you should ask when determining whether someone is ready to lead. The order here may seem counterintuitive, but in my view, skills and tools should be the last element to review on your checklist of whether to hire or promote someone. Even if your manager is equipped with the right tools, if they don't want to lead or don't have the right incentive to lead, you've set them up to fail. Tools and skills can be provided and developed, but they'll work only if the manager wants to grow and already has the structural support to do so.

If your managers don't have the tools and skills for effective management, there's a simple solution: Invest in their development. You can start small and focused. The four most important skills any leader can develop are these: to listen with intention and attention; to ask powerful questions; to be open, honest, and direct in their communication; and to hold critical conversations. Managers who practice these skills daily can motivate, evaluate, and lead their teams successfully.

To set your managers up for success, make sure they have the bandwidth to not only do the work you're asking of them but also time to manage a team of people and work on themselves as leaders.

WHAT'S THE POINT?

Finding the right manager for your growing team is crucial to supporting the growth of your organization. To really get it right, this requires exploring the manager's desires, taking a serious look at your incentives and performance metrics, and then assessing their leadership tools and skills.

Since you've made it this far and are still reading, you are likely one of those leaders who is willing to do the work it takes to build a truly great team. Congratulations! You are already in rare company; most organizations don't take the time to be so thoughtful and deliberate about choosing and developing the right people to lead. By doing so, your company has a better chance of success and of being the type of place where people want to work.

TOP TAKEAWAYS

- Choosing the right manager can make or break the success of the team and your company, so it's critical to get this step right.

- Avoid simply promoting a top performer into a management role. You'll end up losing a top performer and creating a team of employees frustrated with their lack of quality leadership.

- When hiring or promoting a manager, first check: Do they want to lead? Do you have the right metrics in place? Do they have the skills to lead others?

- The desire to manage people is the single biggest factor in whether a potential hire will develop into a good leader or not.

- Include at least one team-leadership metric into your assessment of a manager's performance to ensure they are incentivized to manage their people and not just accomplish their other work tasks.

- Invest in helping your people develop the skills to be better leaders.

ACTION ITEMS

- Use the "Three Questions for Hiring Right" checklist on page 22 to determine your next management hire or promotion.

- Complete the "Identify your individual contributors" activity from page 24.

REFLECTION

- What structures or processes do you need to change to better support your managers?

Chapter 2

WHAT MAKES A LEADER GREAT

*"A leader isn't good because they're right;
they're good because they're willing to learn."*

—General Stanley McChrystal, US Army four-star general

Intention: Understand the key actions that make
a leader great.

I f most managers suck, what can you do to make your managers *not* suck? What are the qualities and habits that make a manager a great leader? To explore this question, I looked back to leaders I'd worked for and admired, to famous leaders throughout history, and to lessons shared by other great leaders, including John Wooden, arguably the most successful coach in college basketball history, and Dale Carnegie, author of the best-selling

How to Win Friends and Influence People. I also looked for common themes and cross-referenced these themes against the thousands of leaders I'd worked with. What I found was a clear picture, a set of four consistent traits great leaders almost always shared.

THE ACTIONS OF A LEADER

A great leader inspires their team to take action. They strategically and thoughtfully assess those people and their teams and are able to adapt to any situation. They clearly and honestly communicate with their teams and recognize that leadership is an act of service, not an excuse to be served. A great leader understands that without others to help them, they can't get to where they want to go. These factors boil down to four traits crucial in any great manager:

- Motivation
- Evaluation
- Communication
- Service

At first, these traits did not strike me as particularly magical or insightful. But I soon recognized something interesting: It isn't just the traits that we should focus on or even the outcomes these traits help produce. No manager goes to work on a Monday and says, "I'm going to motivate today." That wouldn't make sense, because motivating is not an action; it's not something you do. Rather, it's a by-product of the actions you take and how you treat others.

I've also come to realize that outcomes are not very helpful for leaders wanting to learn what it takes to be a better manager of people. As human beings, we spend so much of our time, energy, and attention on outcomes. We might, for example, be focused on closing a million dollars in sales in the next month, which—don't get me wrong—is important. But in order to close the deal, there are key actions that reliably lead to meeting the sales goal you desire; those actions, rather than the outcomes themselves, are the important part.

The same is true for leading. Instead of spending our time focused solely on the outcomes great leaders produce, we need to put more energy into the actions that drive the outcomes. If we can figure out these actions, we'll have a better understanding of the steps needed to develop powerful leaders on our own teams.

So what actions drive leaders to be seen as master motivators, powerful evaluators, expert communicators, and servant leaders? In focusing my attention on the actions great leaders took, I noticed each action was simple but not easy to do. And the great leaders were consistent in taking these actions; they repeated them over and over again, almost as if the actions were a natural part of their daily life. They weren't something the leaders did to produce a one-time outcome; they were habits.

THE HABITS OF A LEADER

Underneath each of the four traits of successful leaders, I identified four essential habits they practice:

- They listen with intention and attention.
- They ask powerful questions.
- They communicate openly, honestly, and directly.
- They hold critical conversations.

Listening with intention and attention

To be a master at inspiring others to take action, you must first listen. When you take the time to have a real conversation with an employee, to show an interest in their work and life, you help them feel seen and heard as a human being. In this, you gain valuable insights into their needs. It gives you the opportunity to support their growth in ways beyond simply providing a raise or job promotion. You motivate them.

Asking powerful questions

Instead of assuming they already know the only correct answer to a question, the best leaders recognize their own minds are naturally biased. To be a powerful evaluator of people, situations, and teams, a leader must be open to new ideas and curious about what they don't know. They challenge their own assumptions by asking questions of themselves, of their people, and of the situation at hand. These powerful questions evoke clarity for the leader, create greater possibility, reveal new learning, and generate action for themselves or their team—all of which help a leader make better, more strategic business decisions.

Communicating openly, honestly, and directly

Being an expert communicator takes more than simply saying what you see. It requires the leader to create a foundation for their people, one built on psychological safety and clarity on where they're going and how they work together to get there. Laying this foundation affords a manager the freedom to be open, honest, and direct with their people. In doing this, they create and cultivate a culture of learning—a place where, instead of worrying about company politics, the team focuses on moving toward a shared vision. This creates a natural effect in which the team and company move more efficiently and rapidly toward desired outcomes.

Holding critical conversations

Being a servant leader starts with the understanding that feedback is a gift. Until your managers truly believe this statement, serving others will be a challenge for them. They may be scared to tell their people the hard truths, afraid of how their team will react, and afraid the team member won't recover or that they'll present the feedback as criticism rather than an opportunity for learning and growth. I've chosen the word *critical* here for a reason: A critical conversation is both a conversation that is necessary and one that provides (constructive) feedback. How you deliver a critical conversation and the way you approach the situation can significantly affect the performance of an individual, group, or the entire company. To hold critical conversations where stakes are high and something must change requires tact and grace. By developing this habit, leaders enable their team to move quickly from a problem to productive action.

WHAT'S THE POINT?

Instead of looking at the outcomes leaders produce, we need to dig a layer deeper to look at the actions driving the outcomes. In doing this, we get a clearer picture of what it takes to be a powerful leader ourselves and the skills we need to empower in our managers.

Having said all this, know that it's rare to find a leader who practices and follows all of these habits. In fact, Gallup's 2017 State of the American Manager study shows that fewer than one out of every five managers exhibits the skills of great leaders.[1] If these habits are what drive business success, why do only one in five leaders embody them? I would argue that it's not due to a lack of knowledge. With thousands of leadership training programs and even more books on leadership available to us, the real gap lies in taking the knowledge and moving to action. This is where we will focus our energy for the rest of the book.

TOP TAKEAWAYS

- Great leaders are masterful motivators, powerful evaluators, and expert communicators. They understand that without others to help them, they can't get to where they want to go.

- Instead of spending our time solely focused on the outcomes great leaders produce, we need to put more energy into the actions that drive the outcomes.

- To be a master at motivating others, you must first listen.

- To be a powerful evaluator of people, situations, and teams, a leader must be open to new ideas and curious about what they don't know.

- Being an expert communicator requires the leader to create a foundation for their people, one built on psychological safety and clarity about where they're going and how they work together to get there.

- Being a servant leader starts with the understanding that feedback is a gift.

ACTION ITEMS

- Look at your team of managers. How many of them have mastered all four traits of good leaders? How many of them are lacking in one or two of these traits? List what you can do to help them enhance each of the four habits.

REFLECTION

- How does identifying the four habits of a great leader affect the way you will support your team?

Chapter 3

HOW HABIT FORMATION WORKS

"There are no secrets to success. It is the result of preparation, hard work, and learning from failure"

—Colin Powell, retired US Army four-star general and politician

Intention: Learn what it takes to move from knowledge to action.

M oving from knowledge to action is hard. Even when there's a desire, an identified need, and the training to change, putting this change into action on a daily basis is challenging. Most of us want to succeed, so it's hard to try something new; we generally know that, in trying something new, we will fail or at least stumble. It's hard to feel as though we're not succeeding or making headway and persist anyway and try doing it over and over again.

That's exactly why moving from knowledge to consistent action—why habit formation—is so hard. It's not sexy, and it doesn't happen overnight. There is no magic pill or secret trick. And while the process is simple, it's certainly not easy. Creating and incorporating new habits into our life require us to do the work and to be both consistent and deliberate so that we can learn and improve from each of our mistakes and successes. Somewhere along the way, the habits start to take hold. I'll show you how.

WHY MOST TRAINING PROGRAMS FAIL TO DRIVE ACTION

In traditional company training, you have one- or two-day-long workshops in which, if you're engaged, you'll increase your knowledge. You'll learn several key insights and be excited to implement the five to ten new skills into your leadership toolkit immediately. Inevitably, though, you won't be able to put all of these new items into action. After two or three weeks, you might remember the concept but not how to implement the idea, and you'll be lucky if you retain even two of the ten key points from the session.

According to McKinsey & Company, "adults typically retain just 10% of what they hear in classroom lectures."[1] That's just retention—keeping the knowledge in your brain. Imagine, then, the percentage of information that typical adults actually take action on. That's likely only a very small percentage. Cramming all the key learning into one lengthy training session makes logistical sense, but it greatly restricts learning retention, not to mention implementation.

Training should give your leaders new skills and help them change their behaviors—to go from being a top individual contributor to a leader of people. As a leader, their success is dependent on the success of the people they're leading. It's quite a shift in perspective from sales metrics or project deadlines. Building and practicing those skills and implementing significant changes in behavior require consistent effort and commitment—and, above all, time. Simply learning what to do over the course of one or two days or even every quarter doesn't lead to people acting differently in the long run.

HABIT FORMATION AND THE BRAIN

Our brains aren't wired to adopt a new habit quickly. No matter how good and engaging the presentation is, habit formation takes time. It occurs only when a new action, such as listening with intention and attention, is practiced over and over. Each time you practice listening in this new way, neurons in your brain fire and create a new neural pathway. The more you practice, the stronger the neural pathway becomes and the easier it is for you to make the new skill a habit.

Imagine you are walking through a field of ten-foot-tall grass. You know you want to get to the other end of the field, but you have no idea how to get there. Forming a new habit is like walking straight into the field, without a map or a path to follow. Once you walk in, it can often be scary, overwhelming, and tiring.

But eventually you will find your way out and onto your new path. Although the first trip through the field was hard, the more often you take the path, the more you mat down the grass, the more signs you put along the route, the easier it becomes for you to take the path—the more habitual it becomes.

The neural pathway for a new skill can be created or rediscovered in one session, but for the pathway to be strengthened, you need to practice deliberately, in a way that is purposeful and systematic. You have to do the work and get feedback on how it went so you can analyze the outcomes and learn from each practice attempt. Role-playing with peers is a safe way to start, but it doesn't replace the real thing. To practice effectively, you'll need to implement the new skill in a real-life scenario—and that's also how you'll have to reinforce this skill with your managers. Only when applied in the real world will you start to get the genuine feedback you need to validate, adapt, and adjust your mental model of what your new skill looks and feels like.

Real-world practice doesn't usually go as planned. It's highly likely that something will go wrong or get off script, and that's when you'll really get to learn. It's like trying to ride a bike for the first time; you're going to fall, and in falling, you learn. When this happens, it's important to reflect on what went wrong, what could be improved, and what you can carry over to your next attempt. If you take this approach, you'll be able to adopt the skill as a new habit, and it will serve you well in business and in life.

A PROCESS FOR HABIT DEVELOPMENT

Since I know you're committed to challenging the status quo, to achieving results, to giving your leaders the tools and skills to transition from individual contributors to powerful leaders, here's the process we will use throughout this book to maximize the probability of habit formation in yourself and in your managers. (You can also use this to structure your own training to optimize action.)

Phase 1: Learn

In the learning phase, you're absorbing insights, information, and research around the new skill. You'll learn about the common pitfalls for the habit, what works, and why the habit is crucial to becoming a powerful leader. Learning the skills, why they are valuable, and how they theoretically can be applied to the workplace is key. It's the context, the reason to keep paying attention.

This is where most training programs spend 90% of their time. I suggest spending only 10% of any training session on the teaching and knowledge-building phase. It's simply not as important as the application.

Phase 2: Apply

In the application phase, leaders practice applying their new habits; it happens during in-session application and through real-world application.

In-session application occurs in the moment when the leaders learn a new skill. It's key to put the skill into practice right away. Ideally, you'll spend 80%–90% of the time applying the new skill with your managers and reflecting on how it can be improved. By doing this, you'll walk with your leaders through the field of grass enough times that it's easier for them later to take over, to practice on their own. In this phase, we are activating the neural pathway and strengthening it.

You can simulate real-world application of the skill in a designed homework assignment or activity to make it easier for your leaders to trigger their new pathways. Applying the new skill outside of the safety of the training brings a whole new element to learning. It's no longer structured. It can take a leader out of their comfort zone because they are now asked to take the path through the field completely on their own, which is exactly where growth occurs.

As you've seen already, I'll give you action items and activities to do and to share with your team. Only in doing these activities will you begin to get out of your comfort zone, practice the skill, and strengthen the neural pathway. If you're thinking, *This is great to use for my team, but I don't need to do the activity*, you'll find it much harder to execute. It's easier to deliver something you can empathize with and have experienced yourself. It builds a stronger connection in your brain than knowledge alone can.

Phase 3: Reflect

Reflection is the component that's most often skipped. When we try a new skill with a team member and it backfires or is painful or embarrassing, we might say, "Well, that didn't work." But that crucial moment of discomfort is actually your opportunity to learn. What worked? What didn't? *Why* didn't it work?

In the work we do with leaders at Raise The Bar, we structure in a coaching session precisely at this point. It's a time for the leader to reflect on what worked well and what could have been done better. If we miss this phase, it can halt the habit from forming altogether.

During a reflection session, my client Leila was explaining how her homework was a total and utter disaster. She held the critical conversation she'd been fearing for weeks with one of her employees, and it completely blew up in her face. She was not only upset about the incident but also discouraged about her ability to lead. I began by asking her to reflect on what specifically about the conversation hadn't worked and what she learned from it.

After rolling out a new internal ordering policy, Leila noticed her employee Kira failed time and time again to follow the new guidelines. At first, she thought Kira was making an honest mistake; but after a few weeks, Leila internalized the failure, telling herself that Kira must be purposefully disregarding the policy. When Leila finally approached Kira about the issue, she tried to let go of this bias but ended up asking Kira to explain what it was about the new policy she disagreed with. As soon as Leila heard the words come out of her month, she realized she'd made an assumption that Kira had knowingly disregarded the policy. What she got back was immediate defensiveness from Kira. It took a few minutes, but eventually Leila was able to more clearly state the issue and learned that Kira had simply been misunderstanding how to follow the guidelines.

What started out as a disaster actually wasn't so bad. In fact, Leila left realizing that, with a few tweaks in how she had set up the meeting and laid out the situation to Kira, she could have had a really productive critical conversation. She realized that, although it had been a painful meeting, she did get the outcome she'd been hoping for: Her employee felt heard, understood what needed to change, and was willing to make the change.

Had Leila not taken the time to reflect, she likely would have avoided her next critical conversation until her inaction similarly blew up in her face and it could no longer be ignored. Instead, she left with a better understanding of what worked and what didn't, of what she should do differently next time, and an appreciation that the sooner she had these types of conversations, the better it would be for all involved.

The reflection phase serves two purposes. First, it holds the leader accountable to completing their homework and taking the pathway through the field of grass outside of the training. Second, it allows the leaders to assess and evaluate how they did and how they can apply the new skills better in future interactions.

They won't perfect the delivery of a habit on their first attempt, so this phase is important to reemphasize how habit adoption is a learning process. Even though the leader is not actually practicing the new skill in this phase, the act of reflecting nevertheless triggers the newly created neural pathway and sends the leader through the field of grass a few more times. By the end of this phase, a leader will have visualized, practiced, and reflected on a singular skill hundreds of times, making a new pathway in the grass and moving from a skill to a habit adopted.

The learn-apply-reflect model is designed to get your leaders practicing skills and putting them into action. The quicker and more frequently a leader can take their new skill, apply it to a real-life situation, and dissect their performance of it, the quicker the skill becomes a habit.

WHAT'S THE POINT?

Culture is the sum of all the actions in your organization. Changing an organization's culture requires changing the behaviors and actions of your leaders—the people who have the biggest impact on the actions of your entire organization. It starts right here, by working with your leaders on adopting the habits that will make your organization succeed.

TOP TAKEAWAYS

- Creating and incorporating new habits into our life require us to do the work and to be both consistent and deliberate so that we can learn and improve from each of our mistakes and successes.

- According to McKinsey & Company, adults typically retain only "10% of what they hear in classroom lectures." Now think of how much of that 10% we are likely to take action on—it's a very low percentage. Learning in a one- to two-day training is not sufficient to drive sustained change in behavior.

- Behavior change occurs when a new action is practiced over and over. It's like walking through a field of grass. The first time through the field, you're creating a new path; each time after, you're matting down the path more and more while also putting signs up along the route, making it easier to find and take the path.

- The first phase of habit formation is learning, where you learn insights, information, and research around the new skill. Spend only 10% of any training in this phase.

- Phase 2 incorporates putting your new learning into action, through practice in the training session and in the real world.

- Don't forget phase 3! It's where you reflect on how your practice went. What worked? What didn't? What needs to be changed for next time?

- To turn a new action into a habit takes visualizing, practicing, and reflecting on a singular skill hundreds of times, thereby strengthening the new pathway in the grass until your leader can take the path without thinking.

ACTION ITEMS

Take stock of your current training programs (either internal or external client trainings).

- What phases from the learn-apply-reflect model are you currently implementing?

- What phases are missing?

- What changes would you need to make to ensure better adoption from the training?

REFLECTION

- What's one thing you can do in the next week to increase the impact of your training?

PART 2

BUILD BETTER LEADERS

It's time to shift focus from the macro level of creating the processes and environment where your leaders can thrive to the micro level. I'll share key information and applicable strategies for developing the four key skills that will make you and your managers more powerful leaders.

As we move on to part 2 of the book, we'll address the four key leadership habits in more detail. At the end of each chapter, there'll be activities for practical application. I suggest setting the book down and putting the activities into practice, then answering the reflection questions that follow. If you don't want to stop reading, set a reminder or schedule the action on your calendar so that while you read, you can still be practicing the habits of a leader with your team. We want to get those neural pathways firing!

Chapter 4

LISTEN WITH INTENTION AND ATTENTION

"The most basic and powerful way to connect to another person is to listen. Just listen. Perhaps the most important thing we ever give each other is our attention."

—Rachel Naomi Remen, author and professor

Intention: Listening is a choice. If practiced, it can transform your impact as a leader.

We think at about 1,000–3,000 words per minute, and we listen at roughly 125–250.[1] This means listening is inherently hard. It's built into our physiology to be difficult. It also means that, before we even get a chance to begin developing this habit, we already have a listening problem. Yet most people believe they are already good listeners, even though they've not spent significant time actively training this skill.

How many hours have you put into deliberately practicing the skill of listening? When was the last time you recorded yourself, reviewed it, and received a critique on your listening?

We've spent a considerable amount of time deliberately practicing the skills of reading and writing through years and years of schooling. Then we get to the crucial skill of listening. Looking back at your education, how many years have you spent training this critical skill? Likely none is my guess.

Until I went through coaching training to become an International Coaching Federation (ICF) certified coach, I'd never practiced this skill in any deliberate way outside of attending a workshop on active listening, reading a book, or watching a TED talk. Knowing *how* to listen is a whole lot different from listening well. Building your knowledge around what active listening is and should look like doesn't necessarily make you good at active listening.

Listening is hard, and we've likely not practiced or trained this skill properly, which is why most people suck at listening—and also why most of us go through each day of our lives not being truly heard. Where there is a collective problem, however, there is also an opportunity. If you can improve your ability to listen a little bit, if you can listen to an employee and make them feel heard, it can have a profound impact.

LISTENING DRIVES MOTIVATION

In a 1963 study, Harvard professor Robert Rosenthal, with the help of elementary school principal Lenore Jacobson, conducted a study at an elementary school in California to understand the impact of a teacher's expectations on student performance. To do this, Rosenthal and Jacobson gave each student a general abilities test and then labeled certain students as academic bloomers. These bloomers, they told the teachers, were expected, on the basis of their test results, to achieve greater academic success. They then told the teachers which students had been identified as bloomers and which had been identified as nonbloomers (the control group). Unbeknownst to the teachers, the bloomers had been selected completely at random, with their test scores having no bearing on their bloomer label. Rosenthal and Jacobson wanted to see if the teachers' treatment of certain students based on their expectation of the student's capability would have an impact on the student's performance. At the end of the study, all of the students retook the general abilities test, and the results were profound.

What Rosenthal and Jacobson found was that the students randomly labeled as bloomers achieved significantly higher scores than the students who were not labeled as bloomers. The students' success, they discovered, was not correlated to their general ability score; rather, their success was determined by the label they had randomly been assigned by the researchers.[2]

How does this happen? It can be explained by the Pygmalion effect, which highlights how your belief in someone else leads you to act differently around this person. Your actions, in turn, affect their belief in themselves, leading them to take action based on those beliefs.[3]

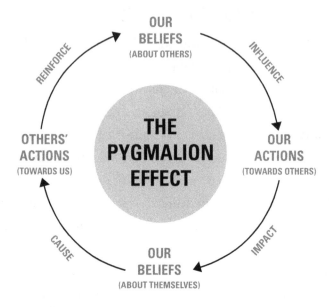

Explained more clearly, by believing certain students had high potential, the teachers gave their energy, attention, and intention to those supposedly better students. They provided more help and gave extra feedback, because they knew it would go further with these high-potential students, the bloomers. The lesson that can be taken from this study is the importance of treating all of your people like high potentials, setting high expectations for everyone. It's not the label of high potential that increases performance; it's showing your employees you care.

Sustained motivation over the course of months and years does not come from a sales competition, a rah-rah speech, a ping-pong table, or free lunches. It comes when you show people you care about them as human beings. It comes when you understand who they are and recognize their hopes and desires. This happens when you listen to your team members, when you are intentional about being there to hear them, and when you give them your full attention.

Listening with intention and attention affords you and your leaders a tremendous opportunity to lead on a whole new level—to truly hear your employees and your team. If you can show them you care and make them feel heard, you'll not only help them connect to you and to their work, but you'll also motivate them to give their extra discretionary effort to you and your company.

THE IMPACT OF *NOT* BEING HEARD

Scott was twenty-six when he reached out to me because he was not satisfied with where he was in his career. He was working at a young tech company that was experiencing explosive growth. The company had an influx of capital, a ping-pong table, flexible work hours, and a fun atmosphere. But Scott was not content.

Unlike most employees who simply disengage and eventually leave when they are not happy, Scott took steps to engage in his career. He hired me as his coach and was willing to throw himself into open, honest, and direct conversations with his managers about his future at the company. When he brought up his growth and development to his boss, Scott felt as though she didn't have time to care about him. She had too much going on and wanted him to go along with the company's plan. Even though their eventual plan included a promotion for him, it meant continuing down a path that Scott was clear he didn't want for his life or career.

After several conversations, Scott felt as though his boss hadn't heard him at all. It was as if he were merely a cog that could easily be replaced by anyone. On the same day Scott received his promotion, he quit. He gave up the opportunity to make more money and have more stock options in order to take another job, one where he felt he could build the skills most relevant to his desired career growth.

Scott's company failed to hear and understand the desire of their high performer. Instead of celebrating top talent moving up in their organization, they were unwittingly hosting an exit interview. This led to their loss of a talented employee who had energy and desire to give more. It also led to a disruption in their work and the need to find, hire, and train another suitable candidate.

When your managers fail to listen with intention and attention, you run the risk of alienating your people. Listening to your employees' needs and goals will give you the opportunity to plan and potentially adjust their path forward in a mutually beneficial way, rather than deciding a path for them without their input—or worse, ignoring their input altogether. If, instead, you practice listening with intention and attention, you'll save your company time and money that you would have spent on rehiring for a position, and you'll create relationships with your employees that will not only make them stay but will motivate them to work harder.

NOTICE YOUR INNER DIALOGUE

The very first thing to do when trying to build the habit of listening with intention and attention is to get clear on what holds you back from listening to others. Listening is a conscious act. How do you approach listening to someone else? What runs through your mind during the course of a conversation? What conversations do you have with yourself while someone else is talking to you?

When you think you're listening, your brain may actually be working overtime searching for counterarguments or ways to direct the conversation back to your desired outcomes. That's not listening. It's more like waiting for your turn to speak: You can't hear what they have to say. And others notice.

We all have internal conversations, but few of us pay attention to them well enough to manage them. If you listen first to yourself, you can regulate your inner dialogue, allowing yourself the ability to truly listen to others. What can you learn about your inner dialogue, and how can this help you become a better listener and leader?

Noticing and accepting your inner dialogue is the first step to becoming a better and more powerful listener. By developing an awareness of the sheer fact that thoughts are constantly running through your brain while you're trying to engage in a conversation, you'll realize you have the chance to do something different. With awareness comes the space to choose what we bring to each conversation. The power of listening with intention and attention comes from being fully present with another person, which can't take place until you are aware of yourself and your inner dialogue.

Here's an activity you can use to test yourself on this skill.

ACTIVITY: BEING IN SILENCE

1. Find a partner.
2. Sit directly in front of your partner so that you are facing each other with your knees almost touching.
3. Set a timer on your phone for three minutes and then put your phone facedown, near you, and on silent mode.
4. Stay silent with this other person for the full three minutes.

What thoughts ran through your head during this time? Did you look around the room? How many times did you think about the alarm and hope it would go off? Did you notice how uncomfortable the silence was? This is your inner dialogue. It's where 90% of every conversation occurs—within your brain. Even if you're thinking, *This guy is crazy; I don't have an inner dialogue!* you are engaging with your inner dialogue at this very moment.

YOUR LISTENING BLIND SPOT

Remember the field of grass we walked through on our way to creating a new habit? Imagine you're back in the field, making your way through the ten-foot-high grass, pushing it aside as you stumble through the field, no longer certain of where you're going, when you notice a paved pathway off to your left. You can see the pathway doesn't lead to where you want to go, but it's there and you're tired, and it's easier than continuing through this endless wall of grass.

The paved pathway is your blind spot. A blind spot is a habitual pattern, either a thought or behavior pattern in your life that gets in the way of you creating a new habit. It's a path you've likely taken millions if not billions of times throughout your life, which is why the path is so well paved. It's comfortable and easy, but it leads you away from where you want to go.

Your blind spot might seem like a bad thing; it's not. It's probably helped you get to where you are. We all have them, although we are typically unaware of them; that's why they're called blind spots.

However, your blind spot also holds you back from greatness. You must notice it to become aware that you're on the wrong path. Once you notice, you can refocus on where you want to go: adopting the new habit and getting back into the field.

We each show up with a tendency we fall into when listening to others. Some of us listen to connect ideas; some of us listen to solve a problem; others listen to figure out what they are going to say next. Each of us listens *for* something, *to do* something. This is your listening blind spot.

For me, it's listening to connect. In each conversation, I listen to see what connection I can make between what the person is saying and something I know in my life, regardless of its relativity to the conversation at hand. I'm constantly looking for key words or ideas to latch onto as the person is speaking: "You're from Michigan? I know Michigan. My sister-in-law is from Michigan. I did a half-Ironman in Michigan. Have you been to Benton Harbor?" It's been a real gift in my life, because it's helped me make connections by engaging in surface level conversations with almost anyone. I'm able to quickly connect to a place or experience they are sharing. It helps me fit in, to feel liked and worthy.

But it is also the number-one thing that holds me back. It was the biggest barrier I faced when starting my business. I needed to not just make connections and be liked; I needed to provide real value, and that only happens when I shut up, let go of my agenda, and truly listen to my clients.

As a business leader, your listening blind spot is something that's likely helped you get to where you are today, so it's natural to have an attachment to it. However, holding onto it won't allow you to get where you want to go.

Take Yvonne, a client of mine who spent the first eight years building her business, Monarch & Company, from the ground up. As a bootstrapping entrepreneur, she had to solve any and all business problems. After those eight years on her own, she added a business partner, Anna, and other team members, which allowed her to take Monarch to the next level.

I started working with Yvonne and Anna during this new phase of their company's life cycle. In a session with Yvonne, she shared how she and Anna seemed to keep clashing on issues. It was frustrating for both of them, and it held back the company's progress. Yvonne told me she couldn't figure out why it was happening.

It wasn't until I was in a meeting with both that I saw it happen live. A simple question from Anna about setting a target for one of her quarterly goals sparked a blowup. Yvonne looked at me as if to say, *See? This is what I'm talking about.* I paused and then smiled as I realized what was going on.

Yvonne had spent her career listening to solve; it was so ingrained in her way of being that she couldn't determine when someone wanted her to solve a problem, to brainstorm an idea, or simply to listen without taking action.

Yvonne thought Anna wanted her to solve the problem and was frustrated because she wanted Anna to be empowered to solve problems on her own, to take the reins of her side of the business. In Yvonne's mind, Anna was asking Yvonne to make all of her decisions. In reality, Anna wanted to discuss and brainstorm the goal together, because she valued Yvonne's opinion and insights. There was a disconnect between the two partners. Yvonne's blind spot of listening to solve was holding her back from not only hearing Anna but also taking the next step in the growth of her business.

Common listening blind spots are when we listen

- To determine my next steps
- To decide if I should pay attention
- To validate my ideas
- To make sure I'm heard
- To figure out what I'm going to say next
- To prove myself
- To learn the other person's intentions
- To understand the issue
- To make my point
- To help the other person

WHAT IS YOUR LISTENING BLIND SPOT?

All of these blind spots, no matter how honorable they may seem, are still blind spots. They hold us back from being present and listening to the other person. Even if your blind spot is listening to help the other person, you're looking in the conversation for ways to help instead of simply being present, without any agenda.

That's the key to listening: no agenda. You have to be present without a destination and without a determination to make. You must listen to hear the other person.

ACTIVITY: DISCOVER YOUR LISTENING BLIND SPOT

1. What is your natural tendency when listening to others (at work or home)? What are you listening to do?

   You may feel that several of the blind spots listed earlier describe you. For the sake of becoming a better listener, pick one. This is where you will focus your awareness and attention.

   I listen to _____.

2. How has your blind spot helped you in your career?

3. How has it held you back?

4. What impact does your blind spot have on your team?

Bringing your habits to your consciousness gives you the awareness and ability to choose a different course of action.

INTENTION AND ATTENTION

Research professor and storyteller Brené Brown shares a great story about the difference between sympathetic and empathic listening.[4] She relates expressing sympathy to looking at someone (a team member) who has metaphorically just fallen into a deep pit and is scared and overwhelmed, and responding with, "Ooh, that's bad. Well, at least you didn't break any bones." When you listen sympathetically, she says, you aren't truly listening to the other person's needs or feelings. In turn, you call out a silver lining for their situation to make it not seem so bad. Expressing empathy, on the other hand, is about going down into the pit with the other person, seeing the situation from their perspective, recognizing their feelings, and saying, "I know what it's like down here, and you're not alone." It doesn't require you to solve any problem or provide any insight; it's about you being present.

Setting your intention to listen with empathy gives the other person a simple acknowledgment of their situation. It's distinctly different from solving the problem. Instead, it's hearing them, showing them you're there alongside them and you care.

ACTIVITY: CHECKLIST FOR LISTENING

Follow this checklist prior to a conversation in which you know it's important to be present, and to listen with intention and attention.

☐ **Remember your listening blind spot**

continued

Simply being aware of your own listening blind spot ahead of time will help you notice when you are doing it. And when you notice, you can choose to stop.

☐ Remove all distractions

One client, Joan, a senior director at a large national wellness company, realized for each meeting she had with her employees that she was in front of her computer, which made it quite hard for her to be present and focused with her team. So she stopped bringing her computer to meetings. It was that simple.

This step is about removing the distractions that will get in the way of you being able to be present in the conversation. It could mean putting your phone on silent, turning off alerts on your computer, or not having your phone out at all. Even the presence of your phone facedown on the table during a meeting is a distraction for your brain, which is why my phone stays on silent in my pocket!

☐ Clarify the meeting's purpose

Start the meeting by getting clear on the purpose. What is each person trying to accomplish in this meeting? What would success at the end of the meeting look like? By beginning with the end in mind, you can let go of trying to wonder what the point of the meeting is and stay on task with the person and the meeting.

THE STAY INTERVIEW

It's time you put your learning into practice—but how? Holding a *stay interview* is a perfect way. A stay interview is the opposite of an exit interview. Instead of learning about why the person decided to leave your company, it's about going upstream and getting clarity on what will make your employee stay with you and your organization. A stay interview helps you connect with an employee outside of a normal one-on-one meeting, to learn about them and their desires for growth. Take your employee to coffee, on a walk around the block, or if you have a remote team, host a virtual coffee meeting where you're each at a coffee shop in your own respective locations. Your primary goal is to learn about where your employee sees themselves in the next few years and what they want for their career.

Start by asking these two questions, and then build on what you hear:

1. What skills are you looking to develop?

2. How can I support you?

ACTIVITY: THE STAY INTERVIEW

1. Outside of your normal 1-1
2. Start by asking
   a. What skills are you looking to develop?
   b. How can I support you?
3. Shut up and listen

When I discuss stay interviews with leaders, I often find hesitation and fear. They say, "What if I can't give her the position she wants? What if we don't have the growth that she is looking for right now?" Asking these questions doesn't mean you need to give your employee more money or a new position. What it means is that you're hearing what's important to her and where she wants to grow, and it opens the dialogue for you to be a coach in her development.

Notice I did not advise you to ask your employee, *How are you looking to grow?* There is a distinct difference between the questions *How are you looking to grow?* and *What skills are you looking to develop?* When you ask an employee about their desired growth, they'll tell you about the next position they want, the title they're looking for, or the amount of money they want to make. Even if you're the CEO, you can't guarantee this to any employee, since you don't know where you'll be in the next three months as a business, let alone in two years.

Asking a question about growth sets you up to let your employee down. Instead, when you ask, *What skills are you looking to develop?* the focus is now turned on the employee and the skills they need to grow. To answer this question, your employee must first think about where they want to be in the future—potentially their desired position, title, or monetary compensation—but then they have to translate those outcomes to the skills they'll need to get there.

You can help the employee here. While you can't guarantee title, position, or money, you can help them develop their skill sets. You can put the employee in key learning situations, assign projects, allow them to shadow someone, find a mentor, or take a number of other actions to help them build the skills they're looking to develop.

Once you ask this first question, shut up and listen to what they have to say. A common tendency our leaders have during their first couple of stay interviews is confusion, discomfort, and silence from their employee after the question is asked . . . which makes sense. Most employees are never heard, and here you are asking them a question about themselves.

Bruce, a leader who went through our bootcamp training, did this with an employee who told him he'd never been asked that question at work before. Both Bruce and the employee were blown away. Know that your employee may not be prepared for this question. They may look and feel a little uncomfortable with you attentively listening to their response; they may not even have a response at that moment.

I have a challenge for you: Instead of bailing your employee out of the silence, shut up for a minute. Don't time it; just be quiet for a bit. Let your employee gather their thousands of thoughts, and be there with them, allowing them time to think and then respond. By giving them a few seconds, you show you're not going to cut them off, that you truly want to know. When your employee sees this, more often than not they'll start to share gold nuggets with you.

If they still don't know what skills they want to develop, don't let them off the hook too easily. Ask to meet again the following week to have the discussion once they've had more time to think and reflect. After a week, they'll have ideas for you. Don't worry.

All that said, there's an important caveat to this activity. Don't do this if you don't plan to follow through. If you don't have the desire to do the work to support your employee, if you don't plan to help them build the skills, or if you're planning on letting them go next week, don't hold a stay interview with this person.

Also, don't hold only one stay interview. I recommend doing these once a quarter with each of your direct reports. People's lives change, and their perspectives change. What an employee says today will not necessarily be what they want tomorrow.

> **Tip:** Put a process in place to ensure your leaders hold stay interviews quarterly.

WHAT'S THE POINT?

When you take the time to have a real conversation with your employee, you help them feel seen and heard. You gain valuable insights into their needs. It gives you the opportunity to support their growth in ways beyond simply providing a raise or job promotion. You can help them grow today by challenging them to take on skill-building projects.

Even if they don't know where or how to grow, what you've done is create space for them to discover this, to start thinking about their future. You can be sure that the next time you talk to them, they will be better equipped to answer the question.

When you listen, you show your employees you care, and you become a powerful reason for them to engage in their work. Having a manager who is a coach and willing to listen inspires and motivates employees to commit fully to the vision and mission of the team.

Take the time to connect with your people. It's these human interactions that make the biggest impact.

TOP TAKEAWAYS

- Listening is hard, and we've likely not practiced or trained this skill properly, which is why most people suck at listening.

- Sustained motivation over the course of months and years does not come from a sales competition, a rah-rah speech, a ping-pong table, or free lunches. It comes when you show people you care, when you truly hear them, when you listen with intention and attention.

- When your managers fail to listen with intention and attention, you run the risk of alienating your people.

- Noticing and accepting your inner dialogue is critical to becoming a better and more powerful listener.

- We all have listening blind spots, and though they are not all bad, your blind spot is what holds you back from being a truly present listener.

- Holding a stay interview is a perfect way to put your learning about listening into practice right away.

- Listening with intention and attention affords you and your leaders a tremendous opportunity to lead on a whole new level. If you can do this, you'll not only help them connect to you and to their work, but you'll also motivate them to give their extra discretionary effort to you and your company.

ACTION ITEMS

- Identify your listening blind spot; see activity from page 66.

- Hold one stay interview with an employee, see page 69 for specific steps.

REFLECTION

- What did you learn from holding your stay interview? How will it impact your approach for that employee? For your next stay interview?

Chapter 5

ASK POWERFUL QUESTIONS

"Smart people are the ones who ask the most thoughtful questions, as opposed to thinking they have all the answers. Great questions are a much better indicator of future success than great answers."

—Ray Dalio, billionaire investor, hedge fund manager, author, philanthropist

Intention: Curiosity is the secret to unlocking understanding and success.

Every day you show up to work, you are making choices, decisions both big and small about whether to hire candidate a, b, or c; how to respond to a client email; who is the best person to put on a project; whether an investment will be a valuable spend.

These aren't blind choices or decisions you make on a whim. You wouldn't be where you are if you did that. Instead, for each of these choices, you evaluate—whether you're conscious of it or not—the candidate's capabilities versus the needs of the role, the real question the client is asking, the project need, or the cost versus reward of the investment. As a leader, you are constantly evaluating people, situations, and teams. Sound evaluation is indispensable to your success as a leader and crucial to your ability to think more critically about your people, team, and business.

THE PROBLEM WITH ASSUMING

In my early career, I led a team as the director of delivery in charge of rolling out our coaching and education programs to new clients. I'd risen fast in this organization and was arrogant. I thought I had all the answers, and it wasn't until we had a major client rollout flop that I realized I had no one to blame but myself. I didn't know the error of my ways until it hit me right in the face.

At the time, "I got this" was my go-to line when I knew what I was doing and wanted to get Marc, my boss, off my back. It communicated that I had all the information I needed, that I knew my team, and that I could take it from there. It indicated that others should stop asking me questions and let me do my work. I remember being annoyed and frustrated that Marc didn't seem to trust me to roll out this new client. But what I couldn't see was how "I got this" highlighted a major mistake. I wasn't evaluating the situation. I wasn't asking questions. I assumed I knew all the answers, and I was wrong. My assumptions led me to put the wrong team members on the project and not provide enough time for proper customization. We ended up overpromising and underdelivering to our new client. The consequence was the client would likely not buy more from us in the future. My job was to execute these client rollouts, and I had failed. Why?

In a debrief with Marc, he said, "Aaron, when you say, 'I got this' and have no concerns about a situation, that is exactly when I get concerned."

What he meant was that when I stop asking questions, it's because I assume I know what's going to work, which means I stop evaluating potential outcomes and solutions. For someone who likes to move fast and make quick decisions and even quicker mistakes, slowing down to ask questions has been one of the hardest leadership skills for me to learn. I'm *still* working on it.

It's a tendency we all have when we want to take the quick route to get somewhere fast. And it's what holds us back from being powerful, strategic leaders. Powerful questions are our way around this pitfall. They provide a means to mitigate our biases and assumptions and allow us to take a deeper dive into the evaluation of a situation, a person, or a team as a whole.

BIASES GET IN THE WAY

I had biases for how the rollout was going to play out. I'd done it before. I knew what was going to happen, so why should I look further into it?

I wish I could say this was unique to me, but we all do this. Our brains are wired to jump to outcomes, to look for shortcuts.

In the 1970s, Daniel Kahneman and Amos Tversky, two behavioral economists widely known as the founders of modern-day behavioral theory, worked together to prove the different ways in which our brains trick us. In their work, which Kahneman would later win a Nobel Prize for, they found how as humans we are not as rational in our decision making as we might think.[1]

Their work highlighted how we make decisions based on our past experiences and the experiences of others. Many times these decisions are illogical; our past experiences are often a *limited* set of all possible outcomes, yet we see them as a finite set—as all the information for a given scenario. Our brain is programmed to be efficient, always looking for the fastest way to make a decision, so we make a decision based on our limited information instead of seeking further understanding. Even with more time and resources to make a better decision, we can tend to make the illogical one. We systematically make these illogical decisions because they fit a mental model. Often, that mental model serves us and works; but when it doesn't, the mistakes can be huge.

Take football, for example. Many of us have a mental model of what a quarterback should look like. We look at the player who can throw the ball the farthest, has the biggest muscles, or runs the fastest, and we think, *That's a football player; he's going to be successful.* Sometimes that's true, and yet there are plenty of times when our mental models are broken.

Take Tom Brady. He was drafted after 198 other players and six other quarterbacks in the 2000 NFL draft. With a total of only thirty-two teams in the NFL, this means all thirty-two passed up on Brady multiple times in the course of the multiday NFL draft. If you looked at his scouting report, nothing on it indicated he'd be a good NFL player, let alone someone who could become a starting quarterback. He had a poor build—too skinny, lacking the physical stature and strength normally associated with an athlete. He was considered to be too slow and didn't have a strong enough arm to get the ball downfield.[2]

Well, as you may know, this skinny, supposedly weak quarterback has become an NFL legend, making it to nine Super Bowls in his nineteen-year career, and three in a row after the age of thirty-nine, winning six of them in total. Because of his record, there's now, at the start of any given season, an almost 50% chance that a Tom Brady–led team will make it to the Super Bowl. He has the most wins of any quarterback, holds the record for the most passing yards and touchdowns with one team, and is widely considered to be the best quarterback of all time.

And remember, this was the same person who initially didn't fit the mental model that general managers, scouts, and football analysts had of a successful professional quarterback. This mental model caused thirty-one teams to make an illogical decision about Brady's capabilities. With the stakes so high and having ample time to assess a group of players with scouts, video analysis, interviews, and even a weekend to compare all players against one another in the same place, how could this have happened? To me, this shows the true power of a cognitive bias—a systematic pattern of thought that causes us to make inferences about people and situations in a highly illogical way.

One of the most debilitating of these cognitive biases is confirmation bias. That's when we listen only to information that confirms our preconceptions about a person or situation. Kahneman stated that "confirmation bias comes from when you have an interpretation, and you adopt it, and then, top down, you force everything to fit that interpretation."[3] This construction of an idea constrains our future thinking. We limit the list of possible outcomes and thwart our ability to make the best possible decisions for our team and business.

Confirmation bias can be fatal for leaders, limiting their decision-making ability and blindsiding them completely. It's our blind spot to properly evaluating our people, situations, and team.

OVERCOMING OUR BIASES

If our biases so clearly and profoundly impact our ability to make the best decision, to properly evaluate a scenario, what can we do? How do we avoid this pitfall? How do we confront this blind spot?

Like any blind spot, it's not about going to war with it; rather, it's about noticing you have it and knowing that it can get in your way. It's about challenging your assumptions and biases so you can determine their validity. You can only do that when you allow yourself to realize that you might not have *all* the answers and when you start asking powerful questions.

The act of asking powerful questions is the most effective way around these biases. Smart, thoughtful questions can help us avoid the all-too-common miscalculation our brains often make. By asking more questions, you can pressure-test your biases, learn more about a given situation, and gain much-needed perspective, which helps you better evaluate a situation.

ACTIVITY: COGNITIVE BIAS

Consider Linda, a thirty-one-year-old woman, single and bright. When she was a student in high school and college, she was deeply involved in social justice issues and also participated in environmental protests.

1. Which is more probable about Linda's occupation today?

   a. Linda works as a TV reporter.

   b. Linda is a bank teller.

   c. Linda is a bank teller full time but remains active in the environmental movement.

Quick. What's your answer—a, b, or c? And in what precise order do you think them most likely?

Here's the solution: First, ignore how you ranked *a*, as it is irrelevant to this mind teaser. The key is this: If you ranked *c* as more probable than *b*, you are wrong—and in very good company. That is what most people tend to answer when they are given this particular brainteaser. Statistically speaking, it is more probable that Linda is a bank teller, of any kind, than that she is both a bank teller and active in the environmental movement, which is a subset of the whole category of all bank tellers.[4]

WHAT POWERFUL QUESTIONS LOOK LIKE

A powerful question is one that specifically evokes clarity about a situation. It creates greater possibility through its exploration of an idea or person. It reveals new learning to the person who is asking it and generates some sort of action from the asker, the responder, or both people. There are a few key attributes that make a question powerful.

A powerful question is open ended

Closed questions provide a finite answer to a question; they are a yes or a no. They limit your ability to learn from the response, which is why open-ended questions are often much more powerful.

An open-ended question is exactly what it sounds like: It leaves the answer open to a thoughtful response, beyond a yes or no. It also allows for the possibility that the answer will go in a direction you don't expect. It helps you to ask for more information without your biases getting in the way and without influencing the person you're asking.

Instead of asking, "Do you think Jeremy is the right person for the team?" you could ask, "What do you think would make Jeremy a fit here?"

Try starting your open-ended questions with *what* or *how*—not *why*. I suggest avoiding the use of *why* as a question word for two key reasons: First, when delivered poorly, it can come off as sounding accusatory or judgmental to the person you're asking, potentially causing them to become more defensive and thus limiting their response. Second, *why* questions force us to reflect on the reason or cause of our behavior, which can be incredibly hard to do in the moment; it sets off a process of lengthy self-exploration and limits creative thinking. Instead of asking, "Why is hitting your goal important to you?" take an extra few seconds to flip the question to a *what* or a *how* by asking instead, "What about hitting your goal was important to you?" or "How did hitting your goal impact you?" Instead of asking, "Why didn't we think of that earlier?" ask, "What assumptions held us back from exploring that option sooner?" or "How could we avoid making the same mistake next time?"

A powerful question comes from a beginner's mindset

A beginner's mindset helps us avoid our blind spot of confirmation bias. When you ask a powerful question while assuming you already know the answer, you inadvertently lead the respondent to give you an answer you want. When you guide a person toward your own conclusion, your leading questions can turn into a self-fulfilling prophecy.

In order to ask more powerful questions, try to let go of your biases and start from a beginner's mindset. Although you may already have an opinion on the situation you're asking questions about, you can't truly learn more until you believe there is more to be learned. Asking just to ask will rarely yield new or valuable information.

Gino Wickman, the author of *Traction*, says, "The mind is like a parachute—it has to be open to work."[5] I believe this is how you must show up to a conversation. Instead of telling yourself that you already know the answer, tell yourself that you don't (at least not yet). Then, ask yourself what more you could learn and what you still need to know.

A powerful question is clear and succinct

There are many powerful questions that die before they finish. I can't tell you how many leaders I see ask great, powerful questions but then keep tacking on words or sometimes even asking subsequent questions on top of the first. Confusing questions rarely lead to new insights.

When it comes to asking powerful questions, simpler is better. Instead of asking, "Who would you need to be and how would you need to change to make the difference you want with the team?" ask, "What one change would make the biggest impact for your team?" or, making it even simpler, "What needs to change?" Instead of asking, "How can you use your learning from this data, your experience, and your past client conversations to properly extrapolate and come up with the best possible solution for the client?" cut down the fluff in the middle and ask, "How can you use your learning to come up with the best solution for the client?" Or even, "What is the best solution for the client?"

A powerful question comes in context

A powerful question doesn't come out of left field; rather, it makes sense to the situation at hand. This happens when your question is related to the topic you are currently talking about. A powerful question isn't powerful because of the words you use; it's powerful because of the way it affects the other person and creates an opening for change. If you've spent the past thirty minutes talking about a problem but ask a question about a different problem, you're likely not asking a powerful question, because it's completely unrelated, out of the blue, and not within the context of the conversation at hand.

Say you're having one of those difficult conversations with a direct report. They've been struggling in their position, and you want to discuss their team's issue of consistently missing deadlines. You begin the discussion by asking: "What does your team need to meet their deadlines?"

"Frankly, we could use more time," he might say. "My team is having trouble keeping up."

This might trigger a connection in your mind: Your manager's inability to ask powerful questions of his team may be why they aren't improving. This leads you to ask, "And how can we make it easier for you to ask critical questions of your team?"

Although this may make sense to you, it will seem to come from nowhere. It's not part of the current context of your conversation. It also carries your assumption that your direct report's failure to ask questions is the driver of them missing deadlines. A better follow-up question to ask would be, "What's holding them back?" The openness of this question will force your leader to explore *why* his team is having trouble keeping up.

A powerful question is impactful

There are hundreds of questions you'll ask in a day, and only a handful of them will ever be powerful. Not all questions need to be groundbreaking. Some questions are simple icebreakers, and some stay at the surface. These are not powerful questions, and that's OK. A powerful question's purpose is to create insight and allow you to discover or gain clarity as it relates to your evaluation of a person or situation. In a thirty-minute conversation, aim for two to three powerful questions.

It will take some practice. But great leaders ask powerful and impactful questions regularly and intentionally. You'll know it's having an impact when the person on the receiving end of your question pauses or even says, "That's a great question," as this is filler for them to explore their answer to the question. Powerful questions are impactful because they trigger deeper thought and contemplation from the person on the other end.

A powerful question happens in the moment

Probably the most important point to remember about powerful questioning is that you can't plan it! Formulaic questions planned before the conversation won't work, often because when they are asked, they are not in the context of the situation. It's hard and time consuming to plan for all possible directions a conversation might go. Asking preplanned questions often fails to bring about the potential insights or the clarity that a powerful question delivers.

Instead, get clear on the purpose of the conversation and on what success in the conversation looks like to you, and make sure to share this with the person you're talking to. Write it down, print it out, do what you need to keep the purpose of the conversation top of mind. When you do, it will allow you to stay in the moment.

A powerful question often takes a moment to sink in

When a powerful question is asked, there is often a pause before a response. The pause happens because the person being asked the question doesn't have the answer ready to go. They are forced to think about what they want to say as they consider their answer.

I was excited to go through the powerful questions module during my training to become a coach. I'd been anticipating it for a while. My ability to ask those thought-provoking questions was what I felt was holding me back from being a great coach. I came into the training wanting a list: Give me the list of powerful questions, and I'll ask them. What I found during the training was as disappointing as it was transformative. There is no list of powerful questions and no one-size-fits-all script to follow. Instead, powerful questions must happen in the moment.

For the remainder of this chapter, we will focus on how you can become better at asking powerful questions in the moment. It may seem like a tangential idea, but I promise it's not. The steps we'll follow will enable you to not have to think about the below checklist for asking powerful questions. Instead, what I share will allow you to unleash the powerful questions you already have inside you.

ACTIVITY: POWERFUL QUESTIONS CHECKLIST

Is the question

- Open ended?
- Coming from a beginner's mindset?
- Clear and succinct?
- In context?
- Impactful?
- In the moment?

ACTIVITY: THE HOT SEAT

The goal of this activity is to provide you and your team a platform to practice asking powerful questions. I especially love this because it forces you and your leaders to ask questions of real work scenarios you are facing today. In addition to helping you practice, it will also help you and your team solve key people-issues you're facing.

Prior to your next team meeting, ask one team member to come prepared to share a challenge they are facing, one to which they don't know the answer. It usually works best when they type up a few notes and share with the team beforehand. Here are a few tips to guide your team member in their preparations.

- The problem: Use one sentence to describe the problem you are looking for help with.
- What's at stake: What makes this problem so important to solve?
- The facts: What are crucial facts to know about the problem? Describe these in three to five bullet points.
- The purpose: What's your desired outcome? What would success look like?

Give the team member two to three minutes to describe the challenge and what success would look like for them in the given situation in the team meeting. Then share the powerful questions checklist so all can see. Go around the room, with each team member firing away a question of the presenter with the goal of learning more about the problem and, ultimately, of helping the presenter achieve their desired outcome. Avoid asking leading questions. Allow around twenty minutes for this.

Close out your questions by asking each person what they learned from this activity.

Hopefully, they—and you—will learn the power of asking questions versus giving advice and the impact it can have on someone's ability to learn, grow, and make impactful change. You'll also begin to notice what a powerful question looks like. Powerful questions are not formulaic, even when you have a checklist to follow. You can't simply write down your powerful questions to use again later. You have to step into the unknown and live in the contextual moment. It can feel uncomfortable, but the results are well worth it.

CURIOSITY AND STEPPING INTO THE UNKNOWN

There's one surefire way to begin asking powerful questions. There's one trigger that, when activated, opens up your ability to be a powerful questioner. It's curiosity.

Do you want to see a master of curiosity in action? Find any three-year-old, and watch them for an hour. They ask *what*, *why*, and *how* to nearly everything they see in the world around them. They want to know more and do not limit themselves by the societal expectations of what's right or wrong. They just ask.

As we get older, we are trained to lose our curiosity when it becomes clear it's not acceptable to ask all the questions that come to mind. Instead, we go about our days having surface-level conversations, rarely digging deeper with a coworker, client, or even friend.

The secret to asking more powerful questions is digging deeper; it is, to a certain extent, about triggering our three-year-old selves and reconnecting with our curiosity.

I've found riddles to be a great tool for bringing our curiosity back. For example, "What has a head, a tail, is brown, and has no legs?"

As you are reading this, trying to figure out the answer, your mind is swirling with questions and possibilities.

- What kind of animal has no legs?

- Is it an animal?

- What else could it be?

What sorts of things have tails? The series of questions running through your head is your curiosity waking up. It's like the little kid inside you wanting to understand everything about the world.

The answer to the riddle is a penny. Did your curiosity lead you to the right questions to arrive at that answer?

To be able to evaluate people, teams, or situations with greater fidelity—go back to the curious part of you that wants to explore. Instead of restricting yourself, open yourself up and allow your mind to ask any question. More specifically, allow yourself to ask the *powerful* questions. Sometimes, your ability to do so may take priming yourself with a riddle to get you there; but believe that you already have the powerful questions in you.

Here's a set of steps you can use to help you ask powerful questions more frequently.[6]

See

Remember, your mind is naturally biased. There is nothing to do but notice you are biased. By reminding yourself, you're creating an awareness of the biases and will be more likely to see them show up in conversations, allowing you to dismiss the biases in the moment.

Think back to the riddle I just shared. That got your mind flowing. All it takes to trigger your curiosity is letting your guard down, changing your state from knowing to wanting to know. I do this by taking a deep breath in and then slowly pushing the air out, letting go of my need to know. I then ask myself, *What more can I learn here? What don't I know?*

Hear

To hear the other person, you need to be with them, by listening with intention and attention. To ask a question in the moment, you need to be in the moment, so start by listening!

Speak

Trust your instincts and allow the questions to come to you in the moment. If you are truly curious and listening attentively, you don't need to worry about finding the right question; it will pop into your head. Trust your instincts and ask away.

SEE-HEAR-SPEAK: A POWERFUL
QUESTIONS FRAMEWORK

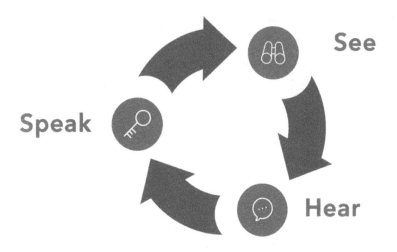

WHAT'S THE POINT?

Powerful questions serve as a means to mitigate your biases and start making more logical decisions. By adopting the skills we've discussed and putting them into practice, you'll find they empower you with a magic tool that helps you learn more about people and situations, uncover elements you might not have been aware of, explore different possibilities, and deliver more impactful outcomes. Powerful questions, if they are practiced consistently, can be your key to becoming a more strategic leader.

TOP TAKEAWAYS

- As a leader, you are constantly evaluating people, situations, and teams. Sound evaluation is indispensable to your success as a leader and crucial to your ability to think more critically about your people, team, and business.

- Cognitive biases highlight our brain's natural tendency to seek efficiency, to cut corners, and in doing so, can cause us to make systematically illogical decisions. These can be disastrous for leaders, limiting their decision-making ability and blindsiding them completely. It's our blind spot that prevents us from properly evaluating our people, situations, and team.

- Powerful questions are our way around this blind spot. They provide a means to mitigate our biases and assumptions and allow us to take a deeper dive into the evaluation of a situation, a person, or a team as a whole.

- There is no list of powerful questions and no one-size-fits-all script to follow. Instead, powerful questions happen in the moment.

- Curiosity is your surefire way to begin asking powerful questions. The secret to asking more powerful questions is digging deeper; it is, to a certain extent, about triggering our three-year-old selves and reconnecting with our curiosity.

ACTION ITEMS

- Complete the hot seat activity (from page 88) with your team.

- Pick one people challenge you're facing, walk through the See-Hear-Speak powerful questions framework (from page 91) prior to evaluating the challenge, and then practice asking powerful questions of the person or situation at hand.

REFLECTION

- What did you notice in observing your team during the hot seat activity?

- How can you use this learning to ask more powerful questions yourself?

Chapter 6

ESTABLISH OPEN, HONEST, AND DIRECT COMMUNICATION

"You have to work hard to get your thinking clean to make
it simple. But it's worth it in the end because once
you get there, you can move mountains."

—Steve Jobs, former co-founder and CEO of Apple, Inc.

Intention: When you create the space, you allow open, honest, and direct communication to flow.

In 2012, Google became obsessed with trying to determine the key ingredients of a high-performance team. In a program called Project Aristotle, it brought together psychologists, engineers, and statisticians to figure out what makes the perfect team. They looked at data from employees across more than a hundred different teams at Google while also performing a meta-analysis of studies over several decades on team performance.

To many at Google, the initial hypothesis centered on the individuals on the team, their ability to maximize their performance, or their personalities and working styles. Google surmised that a proper match of behavioral styles (introverts, detail oriented, strategic thinkers, etc.) and abilities would enable teams to better flourish.

But as Google studied the data, it discovered that the people on the team mattered very little; it didn't matter if a team was full of rock stars, if it was well-balanced with both rock stars and supporting characters, or if it was made up entirely of givers. What mattered consistently from team to team was how the members of the team interacted with one another.[1]

This insight made me smile because it meant that team performance is more under your control as a leader than you may have previously thought. It's not simply about who you have on the team; rather, a large role of your team performance is dependent on how the people you do have on your team connect and communicate with each other. What the team at Google learned from Project Aristotle was that teams that lacked clarity and teams that lacked psychological safety consistently underperformed.

Clarity

Teams lacking clarity on their goals and expectations are not likely to consistently reach those goals or meet those expectations. If I hit a ball at you as hard as I can, odds are high that you're not going to be happy with me. If I now tell you we are playing tennis, you're likely no longer upset with me. Your perspective immediately changes.

Tennis is a game with rules where it's acceptable and encouraged to hit a ball at the other person as hard as you can. The rules establish the expectations of the game—the context—clearly and explicitly. As soon as I give you the context—that we're playing tennis—your expectations change. You understand, at least in concept, the rules of the game we are playing.

In the workplace, we rarely know the rules of the game. One employee thinks we're playing tennis, another thinks we're playing football, and someone else thinks we're playing work. There are no defined rules of the game, because as a team, we've never sat down to establish what game we are playing.

When we don't know what's acceptable to say or to do with each other, when we are confused about what we are doing or how we are doing it, it brings our actions to a halt and makes it hard to get our work done—let alone to collaborate with each other. Clarity about expectations and goals is essential for a team to perform at the highest level.

Psychological safety

Even with clarity, teams also needed psychological safety to perform at their best. Psychological safety is the belief that you will not be punished or humiliated for speaking up with ideas, questions, concerns, or mistakes. When this factor isn't present, going to work and communicating with your coworkers can feel as if you are walking through a series of land mines. Instead of giving someone direct and honest feedback, it's safer to stay quiet and not risk an explosion. The energy we spend trying to tiptoe around one another's assumed land mines takes away from the common goal we're trying to achieve as a team. It is what drives ineffectiveness and inefficiency.[2]

HOW TO CREATE A HIGH-PERFORMANCE TEAM

To create a team that performs, you need people who are willing to be radically transparent with one another and a team that is open, honest, and direct in its communication.

Being open, honest, and direct means that you deliver clear, action-oriented feedback in the moment. This type of live and direct interaction is what allows each individual on your team to operate at their best and to deliver results most effectively for the team. It also means you have a group of people who feel psychologically safe enough to communicate with one another directly. It's the creation of a safe space for people to interact in without fear of consequences.

Creating a team with members who are open, honest, and direct with one another is within your control as a leader. Whether you are the CEO of your company or a manager of your team, you don't need to get your entire company involved to make this happen. You can start today. Open, honest, and direct communication is created when you clearly define the rules of the game, align your team on these rules, and consistently hold yourself and your team accountable to them.

The process starts with identifying your expectations and how you want the team to work together. It seems like a colossal task, but I promise it's simpler than it sounds. When you clearly define how to work with one another and uphold agreements through your actions, you create the space for open, honest, and direct communication to occur.

If you run your own organization, these rules of the game are your company's values, although throughout this chapter, I'll be referring to them as *team agreements* for reasons you'll come to see soon. You will likely want to do this activity on your own and then with your executive team, because their input will be instrumental. It's OK if you already have company values; this activity may enhance what you have or give you new insights to help you redefine your values completely. There is no right or wrong way to go; trust your intuition. Sometimes the values that got you where you are as a business today are not the values you'll need going forward. Organizations, like humans, grow, adapt, and need to change. Embrace a beginner's mind as you begin this activity.

If you are not running your organization and are a leader of a team, big or small, the activity does not change for you, although the perspective may shift. You'll be creating agreements for your team, business unit, or working group. The agreements are unique to you and your team and don't have to be the same as your company's values. The agreements you'll be coming up with are the ways in which your team needs to work together to be at its best. These are fluid and may change as you add team members or as your team's objectives change. As you begin this activity, let go of the need to match these agreements to the values of your company, and start thinking about what your team needs so it can operate at its best.

Step 1: Draft your rules of the game

Team agreements are made between you and your employees about how you will work with one another. They're important because they establish what's OK, what's not OK, and what you can expect from one another. Having a set of common norms gives your employees clarity and also provides a structure for them to feel psychologically safe.

In concept, team agreements are a great idea. But in execution, they're hard to establish. For starters, we aren't always clear on what we want and expect from our team. The most effective way to establish these team agreements is to start by pulling all our ideas together. We'll begin by creating three lists: a list of your expectations, a list of your personal values, and a list of values from other organizations you admire. As we begin the process, I encourage you to write down as much as possible in the early part of this brainstorm. What we are doing is gathering all of our ideas, without judging them as good or bad. Once we have all our ideas captured, we'll narrow down the ideas into a few core team agreements.

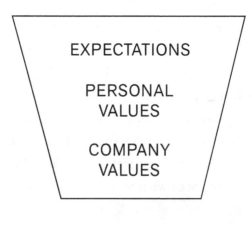

EXPECTATIONS

PERSONAL
VALUES

COMPANY
VALUES

TEAM AGREEMENTS

When you're leading a team, you have expectations for each member, for the goals you are trying to reach, the way to meet these goals, and the dynamics of the team. Some of these expectations are clear, like the goals you have for the team or the key performance indicators (KPI)—for example, we know we need to close $3.5 million in sales this quarter. Some expectations exist that we've never shared with our team members. Other expectations exist, but we're not aware of them—these can lead to confusion. Today we'll start by uncovering some of these expectations that we have but might not be so aware of.

Creating team agreements

To create effective agreements with your team, you'll start by creating a few lists: your expectations of your team, your personal values, and the values other than your own that you respect or believe are important for your team to work together successfully.

List 1: Your expectations

Start by creating a list of all the expectations you have of your direct reports. To help you come up with your list, write down two or more bullets for each question below.

1. How do you know this person is a rock star on your team?

Examples

- He tells me when he's behind on a deliverable before the deadline has passed.

- She asks for help when she needs it.

- He is unafraid to challenge ideas of others, including me.

- She takes risks and is willing to make mistakes.

2. How do you know they're not a fit for your team?

Examples

- He thinks he knows all the answers.

- She makes the same mistakes over and over again.

- She doesn't set deadlines for her deliverables.

- He blames others for his mistakes.

3. What is one thing people on your team do (or one person does) that pisses you off?

Examples

- Show up late to meetings.

- Don't have an agenda prepared for a meeting.

- Don't do what they say they will do.

- Need to be told the same thing ten times to make one change.

4. What expectations do you have that you haven't explicitly shared with your team?

Examples

- Before you say something won't work, do the work and test your assumptions.

- Assume everyone on our team is working together to get to the best possible outcome; no one is trying to intentionally harm you.

- Don't just identify problems; come to me with a plan to solve the problem, even if it's as simple as brainstorming a solution together.

As you do this, list any and all expectations you have of your team. There's no judgment of the expectations. This is filling the top end of the funnel, and these expectations are meant to serve as idea generators for your team agreements.

A lack of clarity about your expectations is your blind spot for establishing open, honest, and direct communication with your team. Getting clear about our expectations, conscious and unconscious, helps us be clearer and, therefore, more open, honest, and direct in our communication. Confusion can arise when we're not 100% aware of what's going on in our minds, including the expectations we have of others. This step is designed to help bring those expectations to the forefront of your mind so you can start the process of creating how you want your team to meet them.

List 2: Your personal values

A personal value is a descriptor of who you are at your core. Once everything circumstantial is stripped away from you, your personal values are what remain. Regardless of how much money you have, how successful you are, or what stage you are in of your life, your values are the core traits that are always true about you. When we honor our values, we feel accomplished and fulfilled. When we disregard our values, we feel frustrated, upset, and unfulfilled. Your personal values are who you are when you're at your best.

The hard thing about defining your personal values is not that you have to go somewhere to find them; they are and have always been inside of you. Personal values are hard to define because there are no real words that can accurately describe who you are. However, this shouldn't stop you from attempting to get close.

ACTIVITY: FIVE WORDS TO DESCRIBE YOU

At the top of a piece of paper, write down the words "I am . . ." Then, close your eyes, put your left hand on your stomach and your right hand on your heart, feeling it beating, pumping blood to all the vital organs in your body. Take a deep breath in, slowly inhaling for five seconds, holding for one and releasing for five. Repeat this for five breaths. After the fifth breath, open your eyes and write down any words to describe yourself. Don't think; just write the first words that come to your mind.

If you pause, you are likely thinking about the words to describe yourself instead of letting them come from within, from your core. If this happens, stop, even if you're only at one word.

Share your list with a close friend, a family member, and a coworker. Ask them to share their opinion on the accuracy of these words describing you and whether they feel the urge to offer a word or two that were missed. You can choose to add their words to your list or not. These words are yours.

Here are mine as a thought starter for you.

I am. . .

- Loving
- Caring
- Funny
- Honest
- Courageous

In listing your values, you'll gain more clarity on who you are at your core. It will not be a surprise, then, that you are at your best in a situation or environment where you are able to express these values freely. On the other hand, the times you get the most frustrated are usually a result of a personal value of yours being suppressed or violated.

Although this activity seems more personal than the others so far, it's crucial to your success as a leader. If you're clear on your personal values, on what fills you up and makes you tick, it will be easier to express this to others, to anticipate it coming, and to plan your team agreements in a way that serves you. If your agreements don't serve you, how will you be able to serve and lead your team effectively?

List 3: Values you admire

Finally, make a list of values that your company currently holds and ones you like from other companies that aren't already on list 2. What's the old saying? *The best compliment you can give is by taking someone else's idea and building on it.* That's how I want you to think about this list. It's where you can look at other team agreements you've seen from brands you like, from competitors you admire, and from mentors you look up to. There are great team agreements all around us, so take a moment to write down your favorites now.

Drafting your team agreements

At this point, you have three lists: a list of your expectations for how your employees should work together, a list of your personal values, and a list of values from your company or others that you admire and may want to include. As I mentioned earlier in the chapter, these activities are about gathering all possible ideas that may be needed to lead your team. Now what we are going to do is narrow down our ideas from all the lists to come up with your team agreements.

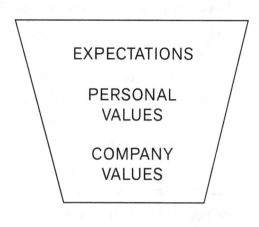

TEAM AGREEMENTS

Look back at your three lists and circle the five most important values and expectations. Narrowing down from dozens to five or less won't be easy. The question I want you to focus on when narrowing down your list, when deciding which expectation to keep and which value to let go of, is this: *What agreements are most important for my team to perform at its best?*

If you lead one team but not the entire organization, your decision can and will be unique to your team. The agreements you choose don't need to be shared by the organization as a whole. Your team has a unique mix of people, with you as their leader and its own objectives within the organization.

It's OK if you want to combine some and if some overlap. Stick to five or fewer. The fewer agreements you end up with, the easier it will be to share with your team, to have them remember, and to hold each other accountable. If you have twenty, you diminish the importance of each agreement. If you have only five agreements, each becomes critical to success as a team.

Defining success

With your agreements in hand, it's critical to define what success looks like for each of them, to be clear about what actions and behaviors match the agreement. Each agreement should have two or three sub-bullets outlining how you will know if an employee is embodying these agreements. By taking the time to define success, you convert an idea that's clear in your head to specific actions that your employees can clearly understand and follow. If you want to keep it as simple as possible and only have a word or phrase with no definitions of success, you'll find quickly that *doing the right thing* may mean something different to an employee than it does to you. For each agreement, ask yourself how you will know if an employee is exhibiting this agreement. What would success look like? What actions would he or she take? This last step is crucial: The more specific you are, the easier it will be for you to hold your employees accountable to the agreements.

On my team, *embracing a beginner's mind* is one of our agreements. Employees who successfully honor this agreement ask tough questions, challenge the status quo, and are curious to find out what they don't know about a given situation.

Here's a full example of what our team agreements look like at Raise The Bar. Notice how each has a detailed set of descriptors, which make it easy for me to hold any team member accountable to the agreement and easy for them to keep me in check too.

Standing in your commitment.
Be clear about the impact you are having on the world and take action from there.

Embracing a beginner's mind.
Trigger your curiosity, explore the unknown, challenge the status quo and ask the tough questions.

Doing the next hard thing.
Get out of your comfort zone, challenge yourself, make mistakes and learn from them.

Acting with authenticity and humility.
Be authentic in the actions you take, in sharing insights and hard truths—allow yourself to be vulnerable.

Having fun!
Enjoy the journey. Laugh, play and lead with love. We are all doing our best to work toward the same goal.

Open, honest, and direct communication in a team setting is triggered when we are clear about our agreements for how we work with one another. By gaining clarity of what the agreements are, we are ready to communicate them directly to our team.

Step 2: Turn your agreements into action

After you've clearly defined your team agreements, the next step is to gain alignment with your team. This is important because the agreements are meant to be used by you *and* your team, not just by you. The hard thing here will be to realize that although the values or expectations were originally yours and you created the agreements, they are not actually *yours*. They will become actions you and your team need to agree on as the best ways to work together. It's important to think of the team as a whole and to think of the purpose of the agreements. You're going to need your team to buy in to them too, and buy-in comes much easier when individuals are able to be involved in the decision-making process. Although you may provide the initial motivation or inspiration, the process will work best if it's a team or joint effort.

One of my clients, David, a sales leader at a Fortune 500 company, learned this the hard way. He did the work of getting clear on his expectations, refined his personal values, and compared them with company values to develop a set of team agreements he was proud of. He enthusiastically shared the agreements with me, and they were good—clean, concise, and action oriented, just what you'd want in your agreements.

David decided to have a little fun with how he rolled them out to his team. As a sales team, they constantly worked in and with contracts—so that's what he did. He put the agreements into a contract, presented them to the team, and had them sign it. The only problem was this: The team didn't agree to David's agreements. There was no room to budge or change anything on the agreements, because they had already been typed out in contract form. Instead of bringing levity to the activity, David brought the opposite: a level of seriousness and tension. Instead of the laughs and sense of unity he'd anticipated, he received silence and realized he'd created a disconnect with his team by leaving them out of the process. Ultimately, the team agreements flopped; and dejected, David gave up on them.

I share his experience as a cautionary tale to help remind you of the importance of ceding the ownership of team agreements to your team when you roll them out. It's critical to show that your agreements are simply a first draft of what you think the team needs in order to operate and function at its best. You need your team's input and contribution to not only make these valuable agreements but also to get everyone on board with the way to move forward together.

David's story also highlights the importance of giving your team time to digest the agreements and upcoming changes. By the time you share your agreements with the team, you'll have spent far more time thinking about these expectations than they have. People need time to absorb new information and won't be ready to fully commit to a new way of working right away, even if they say they are. Give them time to think through the information, and don't ask them to sign anything right away. Instead, invite them to reflect on what each agreement means to them and to come prepared to the next team meeting to discuss them. Through this discussion, you can ensure that you and your team are aligned.

Just because you've defined a set of team agreements doesn't mean everyone on your team will suddenly be open, honest, and direct with each other. You now have to turn these agreements into actions by making deals with the team. This means you achieve alignment on the actions that demonstrate the fulfillment of an agreement. When you and your team align on the agreement and the actions that define the agreement, you have a deal. At that point, you've turned your agreements into actions.

David had a second crack at rolling out his agreements with a new team a few months ago. He made sure to start by getting their buy-in first, and it worked out much smoother for him and the team.

Here are a few steps to getting aligned:

- Schedule two meetings.
- Whiteboard your drafted agreements.
- Share the meaning of each agreement.
- Encourage your team to ask clarifying questions.
- Follow up in writing.
- Make deals as a team.

Schedule two meetings

In the first meeting, provide your team with context. Share the purpose of the team agreements and then roll out your drafted agreements, allowing your team to ask questions and challenge the agreements. In the second meeting, you'll make deals with your team.

Whiteboard your drafted team agreements

Rather than printing out your agreements, write them out on a whiteboard to show their flexibility; you want to communicate that the agreements can easily be erased and rewritten. This will help people on your team feel like an active part of the brainstorming and creation process rather than passive followers of your agreements.

Share the meaning of each agreement

What does each agreement mean to you, and how do you define success? That's the bullet list you created for each agreement. Adding in stories highlighting how a team member held the agreement is a great way to make these actions more tangible for your team.

Encourage your team's involvement

Encouraging your team to ask clarifying questions provides the opportunity for them to challenge the agreements if they don't make sense to them, to dig into each one, and to truly understand what they mean.

Follow up in writing

Send the agreements in a follow-up email, asking people to come prepared to your next team meeting ready to align on the agreements as a team.

Make deals as a team

At meeting two, ask the team if they can commit to demonstrating these behaviors. If they align with the agreements, ask them to commit to exhibiting each behavior. If they can't commit, seek to understand their perspective, and work toward aligning on a revision or new commitment instead. Continue the discussion until all of the agreements are committed to by all of the team members.

If you're the leader, you may wonder why it would be necessary for you to ultimately have to modify any of your original agreements. Don't you get to call the shots? Wouldn't you know what's best for your people? Remember the purpose and intention of the agreements: They are not and were never intended to be only *your* expectations for the team. At their heart, they are a set of guidelines to help your team operate at its best, created by all of you together. If you don't achieve alignment with the team, this won't happen. People don't operate at their best when they feel their boss is unable to truly hear and understand them.

In my experience, it is rare that your agreements will be so off base with how your team feels that they will reject them. Usually, there is one agreement that needs to be revised, reworded, or—in some cases—scrapped. It's much scarier preparing for this, thinking about all the what-if scenarios, than it actually is when you roll out the agreements with your team. If you are open to feedback, willing to make changes, and intend to create a set of common norms for how people on your team treat one another, you'll come out on the other side of this process a much stronger team. Your people will be happier and more invested, and you will have worked together to create the kind of environment that they want to be a part of.

What if you seem to have a good meeting of the minds with your team in establishing the new agreements, but they aren't ultimately willing to follow them in practice? Even once everyone becomes clear on who you are as a team, what you're about, and how you need to work together to be at your best, you'll still find people who don't go along with the plan. I've found that these people are usually the ones on your team who have likely not been a fit for a while. It's not necessarily their fault, and it doesn't mean they are bad people. It simply means their values no longer match the team's. After you have clear language establishing your agreements, you can typically identify these people more easily and help them find a better fit on another team or with another company.

Rick, the co-founder and president of RGE, a rapidly growing engineering company, was in the process of separating from his co-founder and buying back the business. He knew it was critical for his full team to be on board, aligned, and ready to move forward together. My team came in to clarify his company's values, vision, and mission as they were coming out of a transition period and to create a plan for moving forward together. To do this, he first elevated three of his key employees into leadership roles and created a new leadership team to guide the company. When we sat down to craft their values, the process flowed fairly smoothly with Rick and his new team. We'd aligned and were preparing the communication plan to share with the company when Rick paused and asked the group, "What if Sheena and Dejaun don't agree to these? Can we make an exception for them?" We'd just spent hours reaching agreement on the values defining the new RGE. Was Rick now trying to go back on them? What was happening?

Rick was the president of the company, and he, like many of us, still had fears about what happens when someone is no longer a fit. I explained to Rick how these team members would have a chance to align with the agreements, and if they couldn't, he would have to let them know that they were no longer a fit for the organization. Rick knew it was the right thing to do and took the leap of faith that it would work out.

A month later, at their annual meeting, neither Sheena nor Dejaun showed up. They saw they did not fit in the next phase of RGE and opted out on their own. Although I imagine Rick would have preferred not to lose Sheena and Dejaun, the clear language of the agreements ultimately helped Sheena and Dejaun understand what they wanted to work toward professionally and that RGE was moving in a different direction.

When you clarify who you are as a business and team, there will be people who either can't or don't want to make the transition to the new way of working as a team. Expect this. And when it's time, be ready to do the next hard thing you need to do. It will show the power of your words, that these new agreements really matter, and it will make your team and business stronger as a result. Rick and RGE are now coming off one of their best years as a business, a year where they had to buy out their co-founder and yet still nearly doubled in revenue. They're looking to do the same in the coming year. Rick and his team confidently stood by their values and who they are as a business, and it's made them stronger.

Turning your agreements into aligned actions makes sure there is no space for confusion. You and your entire team should know exactly what's expected of each of you. Once the agreements are in place, you've created a space where clarity and psychological safety are not only accepted but also anticipated and expected. Change does not happen overnight. People on your team will likely be unable to change course and their behaviors so quickly. So, as the leader, you'll need to embed it into their day-to-day workflow.

Step 3: Embed your agreements into your day-to-day work

After you have alignment on your agreements, you can start to make them a part of everyday life within your organization or team. They can now be the foundation for the type of culture you want to create, and you'll be able to tell your employees, unapologetically, what it means to work together here. Agreements are not just words that go up on a wall in your office, on your website careers page, or in your employee handbook. To really stick, they need to be ingrained in the actions your people take on a daily basis. This happens only when you incorporate them into your team's people practices—when they become the criteria for hiring, firing, and promotion.

Here are some best practices for incorporating your agreements into your everyday people practices:

Add your agreements to your interview process

Once you assess a candidate to see whether they have the ability to do the job, the next step is to assess them as a value fit. This means asking specific questions and looking for examples highlighting their expression of your team's values. By interviewing for value matches, you'll save yourself the trouble of having to let go of someone who's not a fit for your company months later. Doing this kind of assessment up front also works in the best interests of the candidate, who, ideally, will wind up in a good work situation that is not only aligned with their own values but also makes them happy.

Don't just assess performance KPI; add in values KPI too

Instead of only assessing an employee's performance (quarterly or annually) based on how well they did against their performance metrics or KPI, include a section to assess how they did in light of your team agreements. One easy way to do this is to have employees score themselves on a scale of 1 to 5 (1, *strongly disagree*; 5, *strongly agree*) based on how well they believe they personally live into the team agreements. Then, you do the same assessment of them based on their peers and your observations.

This is a great way not only to make sure that you and your employees are on the same page with their performance but also to show that your agreements really mean something. What gets measured matters, so if you're not continually measuring and assessing your employees and yourself against your agreements, they begin to fade away.

Follow up and follow through

I frequently find myself talking to business leaders who complain about employees wanting to be promoted. They'll say a particular employee is just not ready to be promoted, which I'll begin prodding with these questions: What does that mean? What does the employee need to do in order to be ready? Usually, the response falls somewhere along the lines of this employee needing to more consistently meet the team agreements.

Well, why doesn't the employee know that? This brings us back both to the values KPI in your evaluation of the employee and to open, honest, and direct communication. The employee is probably asking for a promotion because they believe they've lived up to your team agreements and don't understand why you don't see that. Think of your agreements as both a tool and an opportunity. They offer an easy way for you as a leader to point out where growth is needed when the person performs well but is not a fit for promotion. Make it clear what's missing from their performance so you can get on the same page. They'll know what's required to earn that promotion, and you'll have an employee ready to improve for a specific, reachable goal.

This becomes much harder when someone is a top performer but they continually violate your team agreements. When this happens, you must fire that employee; otherwise, you'll be sending the implicit message that your agreements don't actually matter or, worse, that there are some people who are above the rules.* If your employees hear you talk about the importance of your agreements, but you put up with a top salesperson consistently disregarding the agreements, you send the message that it's OK to violate any agreement, as long as you're good at what you do. This does not create clarity or psychological safety, but rather discord and misalignment in your company. Is this the message you want to send to your team?

Note:

---

* Your first course of action with an employee not meeting an agreement should not be to fire. It should be to communicate the miss and give them the coaching and support

they need to meet the team agreement. Rarely should an employee be surprised about being let go, as you should have had several conversations leading up to this final decision where they know what they need to work on and have the support to be successful.

Step 4: Model open, honest, and direct communication with your team

Team agreements are not meant to be used simply as inspirational quotes. To work, they need to be used daily. In the beginning, your team will have to get used to the new agreements—and it's vital to share feedback with them both when they are honoring an agreement and when they're violating one. As a rule, make sure to recognize, call out, and check in on agreements weekly with your team. Open, honest, and direct communication is not a one-time thing; it is meant to be a habit you practice every day. The more often you offer and receive feedback, the better the team can work.

When I think of feedback, I look at sports teams for comparison. Consider Drew Brees, the quarterback of the New Orleans Saints. After each play, Brees huddles up with his team, and they discuss the next play. In the huddle, he's receiving the play from his coaches, gets input from his teammates, and gives them actions to take. They break the huddle and set up for the play, all while Brees is looking at the defense and shouting changes to the rest of the team. At no point does Brees stop and think about how to politely give feedback. He doesn't wait to send a well-crafted email or, worse, wait six to twelve months to tell someone what didn't work on third down with two minutes left in the game. That'd be ridiculous, it'd be pointless, and it'd be too late. So why, at work, do we wait twelve months before giving feedback to our team? How can people truly develop like this or grow in their roles in real time?

When you have feedback to give to a team member, whether it's positive or negative, give it live, and make sure it's actionable. Don't wait weeks or months for a performance review. Share the feedback with them as an opportunity for development or understanding.

Here are a few tips for giving live feedback:

Give it in person, over the phone, or via video chat

These are the highest fidelity modes of communicating, in which it's easy to understand when someone is being sarcastic, joking, or simply asking a question with no intonation. When you give feedback via text, messaging, or email, you potentially leave room for misinterpretation. A rule I stick to is this: If an email is taking me more than five minutes to draft or respond to, I don't send it. Instead, I pick up the phone or walk down the hall to connect with the person live. So many office conflicts would be solved by simply communicating with one another.

One of my clients, Ozzie, the CEO of a fast-growing advertising agency, had two members of his executive team who'd been fighting. Their relationship had been degrading with each passing month, and Ozzie had failed to take action. At one point, Ozzie, frustrated himself, realized that their disagreements were affecting how the rest of their team worked with one another, and he could no longer stand for it. Ozzie looked at the situation, after having both employees come to him to plead their case and hoping he'd side with them, and decided to do the simplest of all actions. He brought them together in a room, shared how they were both failing to hold up their end of their team agreement to collaborate openly, and forced them to talk it out.

Although their desks sat no more than fifteen feet away from each other, all of their arguments had taken place via email. They'd never actually sat down to truly hear one another's perspective. As soon as they did, it was as if an invisible barrier had been removed. Their relationship immediately changed; they were both more ready and willing to work together, to truly listen to one another. They didn't need to agree with the other's perspective; they just needed to hear, understand, and appreciate it.

Open, honest, and direct communication is not about agreeing with the other person. It's about openly communicating disagreements and working together to reach the best possible outcome for the company and for one another.

Avoid using absolutes like always and never

Absolutes add a level of judgment to a situation that likely isn't true and often leads to defensiveness. If you tell someone they always miss a deadline, the thought running through their head is all the deadlines they have hit. Even a positive piece of feedback gets watered down when framed as an absolute. Which of these two statements would be more effective for an employee to hear?

- "Sunil, you always do such a great job!"

- "Sunil, well done going above and beyond to get Eli at SandCare the reports two days early. Eli was so grateful you helped him out of a jam, we're meeting next week to talk about another project!"

Yes, statement two may take a few extra seconds to think about and share with your employee, but the impact is far more profound. This form of specificity makes the compliment more personal and helps your employee feel seen and heard, and shows the impact of their work. Remember, lack of impact is one of the key reasons people leave their company; being specific is a simple way to make sure you share the impact they're having.

This tip is not just about the positive. Even when sharing feedback on something that didn't work, avoiding absolutes will help make it clearer and help the person feel less judged.

The more specific you can be with a piece of constructive feedback, the easier it will be for your employee to know what to do or not do the next time. Instead of telling them to write emails that are more professional, share how the two grammatical errors in their email didn't meet your expectations for emails going out to clients.

Be timely: Deliver the feedback within three days of the incident

The longer you wait to give a piece of feedback, the less effective it will be. Leaders often wait weeks until the time is right, and by then, so many other things have happened that the person you're giving feedback to may not even remember the original event. The sooner you give the feedback, the sooner that person can do something about it.

Share both good and bad

If someone doesn't get feedback, how can they grow, make a change, or continue doing the action you're applauding? Don't share the good and the bad together. Feedback sandwiches just don't work; in fact, they undermine the positive feedback you give and diminish the importance of the constructive feedback.[3] This is related to the last point: Don't wait to combine multiple feedback items; instead, discuss positive actions when they happen, and give constructive criticism when an issue arises that requires it.

Craig Wortmann, a clinical professor of innovation and entrepreneurship at Northwestern University's Kellogg School of Management, first shared this 4-step process with me a few years back. I love the way he's adapted it to make feedback a habit with your team.[4]

ACTIVITY: MAKE FEEDBACK A HABIT WITH YOUR TEAM

1. What's one thing you did that worked well?
2. Here's one thing I think you did that worked well . . .
3. What's one thing you would do differently?
4. Here's one thing I think you could do differently . . .

I use this process after any presentation or sales meeting. We do a quick three-to five-minute debrief following the meeting, during which I'll ask an employee what one thing is that they think they did well. I allow them time to respond and give one focused insight before sharing the specific action I thought they did well. Then, it's a hard stop to let the feedback sit; sometimes, having them write it down is helpful, so they can remember what to repeat during their next presentation. Next, I ask the employee what one thing they could do better. I find that letting the employee share first gives them the opportunity to reflect on their growth area and share an opportunity that I may have been thinking about too.

I love the focus of this model, because it only asks for one thing, not two or five or ten. Although the employee might have five to ten things they could improve on, this approach allows me to narrow my feedback to one item, potentially the most important element for them to focus their growth on. This is also important because the employee would likely be unable to change all ten of their mistakes at the same time anyway. Experience and science on behavior change has taught me this. But when I give one piece of feedback, it gives them a much better opportunity to make a change for next time. It's doable rather than overwhelming, and specific rather than vague.

WHAT'S THE POINT?

Over time, live feedback becomes infectious, and the more you do it, the more others will adopt your model of open, honest, and direct feedback. The result is the creation of a learning culture within your organization, one in which people give and receive feedback in the moment, and it's often the feedback they need most in order to best support their growth and the company's success.

Your biggest barrier to making these steps work with your team is consistency. In business and in life, we are often willing to try a strategy out for a few weeks before we either forget about it or deem it unsuccessful. I see this all too often with leaders. If you think this will provide a quick fix to your team dynamic issues, it won't.

To create an open, honest, and direct team, you must commit to your agreements and consistently uphold them on a daily basis. It will likely take months of consistency for your team to truly understand that these agreements are here to stay and for them to fully get on board with operating by them. Nevertheless, be patient and consistent.

TOP TAKEAWAYS

- Team performance is more under your control as a leader than you may have previously thought. It's not simply about who you have on the team; rather, a large part of your team's performance is dependent on the clarity and psychological safety you create.

- When we don't know what's acceptable to say or to do with each other, when we are confused about what we are doing or how we are doing it, it brings our actions to a halt and makes it hard to get our work done—let alone to collaborate with each other. Clarity about expectations and goals is essential for a team to perform at the highest level.

- Lack of psychological safety and the energy we spend trying to tiptoe around one another's assumed land mines is what drives ineffectiveness and inefficiency on your team.

- Creating the space for open, honest, and direct communication to occur starts with establishing team agreements.

- When you clarify who you are as a business and team, there will be people who either can't or don't want to make the transition to the new way of work as a team. Expect this to come, and when it's time, be ready to do the next hard thing. It will show the power of your words, that these new agreements really matter, and will make your team and business stronger as a result.

- Agreements are not just words that go up on a wall in your office, on your website careers page, or in your employee handbook. To really stick, they need to be ingrained in the actions your people take on a daily basis. This happens only when you incorporate them into your team's everyday practices.

- After you have alignment on your agreements, you can start to make them a part of everyday life. They are now the foundation for the type of culture you want to create, and you'll be able to tell your employees, unapologetically, what it means to work together here.

ACTION ITEMS

- Create your initial draft of team agreements.
- Hold your first meeting to make deals on your drafted agreements with your team.

REFLECTION

- What's been the impact of rolling out the agreements with your team?

- What are you doing to ensure these agreements stay top of mind with your team?

Chapter 7

HOLD CRITICAL CONVERSATIONS

"Courage is not the absence of fear, but rather the judgment that something else is more important than one's fear."

—James Neil Hollingworth, American poet and writer

Intention: Feedback is a gift. Without it, people don't grow.

I still regret the way I managed in my first attempt at leading a team. There was one employee in particular, Jess, with whom I wish I'd had more courage. Jess was underperforming in the most basic sense. She'd not follow through on an agreed-upon deliverable and would miss key assignments. She was good at her job when she did it, but there were many times when she failed to do the necessary work. I would deliberate with myself each time a deliverable was missed.

Should I bring this up to her? I'd ask myself. *But she did this other thing well. Her colleagues had positive feedback about her. Then again, she missed this deadline after I clearly stated when it was due.*

I was afraid to give her feedback. I thought if I gave her critical feedback, she would not be able to bounce back and go out and deliver. I sugarcoated my feedback to Jess, starting and ending each conversation with a positive—dulling the message. I realize now, though, that by not sharing real, honest, and direct feedback with Jess, I was robbing her of an opportunity to see the areas of potential growth she was missing. The more you hold back on sharing feedback and the more protection you give your employee, the more you rob them of their growth. Whether they acknowledge your honesty in the moment or five years later or never, by sharing the harsh truths, you allow someone else the opportunity to learn and to grow. You help not just yourself and the person in question but your other team members and the company, who all stand to benefit from this growth.

Imagine trying to get better at shooting a basketball if you only ever practice in the dark. Without the ability to see where the ball goes—whether it goes in or hits the rim or bounces off the backboard—how would you be able to know the proper adjustments to make? Your work as a leader is to shine the light on the situation so your employees can see the impact of their actions—so they can learn, grow, and get better.

Just because you shine the light doesn't mean your employee will appreciate the light being shined on an area of their work. Receiving feedback isn't easy to do. In developing our training model, I had a good sense of how I wanted the program to look and flow, and I knew it needed feedback and various other perspectives outside of mine to be better. I engaged a colleague, Carolina, to help map out and design our leadership bootcamp course. Throughout the course of our work, I'd ask her for feedback on what we needed to do differently, on what would make the training even more impactful for the leaders we worked with. Each time Carolina shared feedback that forced me to rethink a whole section, rather than make a simple edit, I cringed. Her feedback was valid, and it still hit me like a punch in the chest. Feedback, even when requested, can be hard to receive.

The way I receive feedback is a growth area for me as a leader. I now often follow up a piece of feedback with a thank you, because it not only reminds me that it's a gift someone has given me but also because it lets the other person know I appreciate the gift and want more to come. It doesn't mean I always take it well.

Even when we ask for feedback, the idea of hearing what could be done better in our work or life usually drives defensiveness. If you know your own reaction would be defensive, think about how the idea of feedback, especially critical or negative feedback, might feel to your employees when you deliver it to them. Since we often avoid giving critical feedback, we miss the mark when we do have to have a critical conversation. By establishing a clear set of team agreements, you'll be better equipped to share feedback in the moment. Yet, there are times when feedback is more than sharing what didn't work in the moment, when it requires a conversation.

What's the difference between sharing feedback and having a critical conversation? When you share feedback, it's direct: You share what didn't work and what needs to change next time; usually, the behavior or action desired is fairly black and white. Let's say, for example, an employee schedules a meeting with you and comes in with no set agenda. The direct feedback is, for any future meeting you set, to come prepared with an agenda, because it helps ensure a productive meeting for all involved. That's what giving direct feedback looks like. Now, if the employee continues to show up to meetings without an agenda prepared after you repeatedly set the expectation of coming with one, this is where the situation may transition from feedback to a critical conversation.

WHAT MAKES A CONVERSATION CRITICAL?

How do you know when something an employee did requires more than just sharing what didn't work, when it requires a deeper dive with the employee, a critical conversation? Remember that by *critical*, I mean both vitally important and involving a critique of behavior.

There are four key elements to look for when determining if you need to have a conversation with the employee instead of giving them direct feedback.

Something is at stake

Critical conversations are necessary when the stakes are high for you, the employee, the company, or all of the above. This is when there is a risk of losing a client, missing a major deadline, of delivering low-quality work—when there is some serious risk that needs to be addressed.

There's an impact if nothing changes

What will happen if things keep going the way they are going? If something needs to change, that's when a conversation becomes critical. With my previous example, if the employee keeps coming to meetings with no set agenda, the impact is that we continue to have meetings that aren't productive. More important, it sends a signal that, as a leader, I really don't hold people accountable.

Action is required of both parties

If you're the one holding a critical conversation, you're likely asking someone else to change something. Although this is often the case, change coming from a critical conversation is not one-sided. This one is usually harder for people to understand. If you are asking someone to change something about the way they work, treat you, or interact with a fellow employee or client, something is required of you as well. It might be the way you support your employee in making the change, or it could be how you hold the employee accountable when he or she doesn't make the agreed-upon change. Either way, there is something required of both parties involved in the critical conversation.

It's a conversation

A critical conversation is not a demand, it's not an admonishment of the other person, and it's not an ultimatum. It's a conversation between two people; this means it's two-sided. It means it's not just about sharing your perspective on what didn't work, but it's also about listening to the other person's perspective, about hearing their point of view, and about coming to agreement together. That's why it's called a critical conversation, not a warning meeting or a reprimand or negotiation.

Here is a quick set of questions to ask in helping you determine if you need to have a critical conversation.

ACTIVITY: CRITICAL CONVERSATION CHECKLIST

☐ Is something at stake?

☐ What's the impact if nothing changes?

☐ Is action needed from both parties?

☐ Is it a conversation or ultimatum?

We rarely notice the impact of not having a critical conversation immediately, although the repercussions of avoiding it can haunt us for weeks or months. A client of mine—let's call her Emma for the sake of anonymity—hired her first chief sales officer, Jake, to help her team grow to the next level. Jake was the highest-paid employee on the team, he had experience, and Emma was excited to have him as a part of the team. In the first few months, Emma started to notice in meetings how Jake would not listen to the client's ideas but would deliver what he thought was best. This went against Emma's philosophy of listening to clients and serving their needs. She was irked by these meetings but said nothing. Over the next several months, she continued to notice instances where Jake was not communicating well with the other departments, taking a me-first approach, and taking credit for work his team delivered without recognizing the team. Emma was furious with the way Jake, her top hire, was acting as a leader for the organization.

When I asked Emma if she'd shared this feedback with Jake, she paused, blushed, and doggedly admitted she'd not shared any of it. Instead, she moved Jake off their biggest clients and tried to protect the team from his interactions. She'd been watching from the sidelines as Jake was unknowingly dismantling the culture she had worked so hard to create, too afraid to speak up until, now, she started to see her executive team look at her in a different way. They were all complaining about Jake and wondering why she kept someone on the team who clearly wasn't a fit. Emma finally realized the error of her ways and held a critical conversation with Jake— six months too late. The result of the conversation led to Jake and Emma agreeing on action items to take and, a month later, after he didn't meet any of them, they parted ways.

What was the impact of Emma waiting six months to have a critical conversation? In the immediate term, she paid six months of top salary to an employee whose value didn't match the pay. She had to stretch her other employees to compensate for Jake's limitations, and she denigrated her values by not taking action when Jake violated those values. It wasn't until after she let Jake go that she felt the difference. Immediately, the productivity of her sales team exploded, landing new client deals and delivering great work. She promoted Ranelle, the employee below Jake, to a director-level position and noticed that she didn't need a chief sales officer at all; Ranelle could do all of Jake's work and more.

It wasn't until two months later, though, that Emma took the ultimate blow for her lack of urgency in having a critical conversation. Two months into her new role, Ranelle put in her notice. She was leaving, and when Emma asked why, she said she'd been in talks with a competitor for the past four months. She'd had enough of working for Jake and an organization that promoted selfishness, and she had decided to look elsewhere. Emma not only lost six months of her team producing at a high level, but she now lost a key employee, all because she didn't have the conversation she knew in her gut she needed to have.

What critical conversation have you been putting off?

In this chapter, we are going to walk through the science of human behavior and how the brain reacts to feedback and events. Then, I'll share a nine-step process you can use in order to hold more productive critical conversations. Once you've walked through the process, you'll have the tools, language, and confidence to hold the critical conversation now instead of putting it off. The goal is not only to have the conversation but also to make it as productive as possible—to put you in a position to have a successful conversation. Although I can't guarantee the outcome of the conversation, I can give you tools to achieve the best possible outcome.

ACTIVITY: PICK A CRITICAL CONVERSATION

What critical conversation do you need to have? Write down

one critical conversation you need to have or have been putting off. Write down the situation and players involved in a
brief paragraph for yourself.

Use this situation as your example to follow for the rest of
this chapter. It will make the steps in the process more real
for you, making it easier to take action and learn the skill. In
short, you'll be strengthening your neural pathway for holding
critical conversations.

As we walk through each step, I'll share a story about a critical
conversation I needed to have but had trouble preparing for. It's
actually the situation that drove me to realize there's a better way to
communicate challenges with others.

One incident happened during an account review meeting with
Kevin, the director of accounts, and me, the operations director. We
were walking through a problem with one of our clients, ABC Corp,
who was not happy with what we were doing. Kevin wanted me to
change our processes and operations to serve the client's complaints,
and I didn't want to. This wasn't the first time Kevin asked me to
make client changes that I pushed back on. I didn't see the reason
for the change; instead I saw it as more work for our team with no
better outcome for the client.

Kevin naturally became frustrated and focused on telling me
what we needed to do and how to do it. I suggested we set a meeting
with the client to get to the root of their issue, because I didn't think
Kevin's suggested change would solve their underlying complaint,
causing us more work only to have to change course again. At that

point, Kevin's frustration boiled over and he yelled at me, "Do you even care about this business?"

In response, an immediate rush of self-doubt and anger toward Kevin ran through my head. *Why doesn't he respect me? Why doesn't he trust my ideas or opinions? Why is he so stubborn? He just wants to make sure things go his way. Why doesn't he understand that I'm not just trying to take the easy route?* Unsure of how to respond, I remained silent, and he stormed out.

Account teams and operations teams tend not to get along so well. While the account team is focused on satisfying the client, the operations team is focused on delivering the best product to the client as efficiently as possible. Though these objectives sound the same, they are frequently at odds with each other, leading to a natural tension between the two teams. In our situation, both Kevin and I were trying to set up our company for success yet had different opinions for how to make it happen.

It's clear there needed to be a critical conversation. As the heads of our respective departments, the way we worked together was critical to the success and future of our business. We needed to be able to disagree and move forward from it better. But I wasn't sure where to start. How could I go about having a critical conversation so Kevin would hear me? How could I let go of my biases about Kevin and how I expected him to respond? How could I put myself in the best position to have a productive critical conversation? To do this, I first needed to understand how the human brain works, how we react to situations and to receiving feedback.

THE SCIENCE OF HUMAN REACTIONS

The way we think human behavior works is quite different from how it actually works. For the sake of this discussion, we are going to look at how humans react to a specific event.

When a critical conversation becomes necessary, there is often an inciting incident, something that sparks the need for the critical conversation to occur. It might be an employee showing up late to meetings over and over again, or it might be the way a colleague treated you in front of a client. In my scenario, it was the fight with Kevin. Whatever the incident is, something sparks your response. This is where we will magnify human behavior, specifically looking at the incident and response.

Here's how we tend to look at the human reaction: There is an incident, and then there is a reaction. That's how human behavior works, right? The incident causes the reaction to happen.

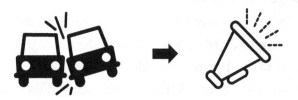

We are often unaware of the many other steps that occur instantaneously following the incident. Let's pull back the curtain to see how human behavior works here. To truly understand how we as humans act, we must first realize that each person sees the world through their own filter—in essence altering the way they see the world around them. It's why you and a friend may watch a movie and end up having very different interpretations and takeaways.

Each of us has this filter through which we see the world. Our filters are made up of our personal values, our beliefs of right and wrong, what we expect from others, and all of our past experiences. No two filters are alike, just as no two people are the same. Your filter impacts the way you see and experience the world around you. In real time, the incident you were a part of is instantaneously received through your filter and triggers an automatic physical, emotional, and intellectual reaction.

Imagine for a moment that you are walking through a dark alley at night and you hear a loud bang. Cortisol and adrenaline immediately surge through your body, activating your physical fight-or-flight response, and as all of your muscles tense in your neck, you clench your fists and get ready to bolt. You're afraid (your emotional response), thinking a gun was just fired and you're in danger (your intellectual response). Your filter tells you darkness plus loud bang equals danger. All of this happens in a split second.

Now, imagine a waiter who works at a restaurant on the same block. He frequently leaves work through the back entrance so he doesn't have to pass by any diners, choosing instead to walk through the alley after his shift is over. He's walking home in the dark down the alley and hears the same bang you just heard. However, for the waiter, there's no adrenaline or cortisol rush through his body; there's no fight-or-flight response, no fear, and no worry of danger. Why? Because he's used to walking through the alley and knows the sound of trash being thrown into the dumpster outside his restaurant and the bang that comes with it. His reaction is completely different from yours because of his filter, because of the way he views the world. It's been colored by his past experiences of walking down the alley at night, of knowing what to expect, so he's not immediately stressed. His filter is different from yours.

This isn't the end of the story, though. Our filter only explains our instantaneous reaction, clenching our fists and preparing to run; it doesn't explain the actions in the subsequent minutes. Do we call the police? Do we move out to the street? Do we hide?

These actions come as a result of our core desires as human beings. If there is one thing that's true about all humans, it is that we have two desires: the desire to avoid pain and the desire to seek pleasure. It's pretty basic, and if you look at why people do what they do, it explains most human behaviors. It doesn't mean that people are logical in seeking pleasure or avoiding pain; it simply means they act most often out of the avoidance of something painful, like having a critical conversation, and toward something pleasurable in the short term, like eating a piece of chocolate. This desire leads us to make a choice about what to do; this choice is often not a conscious one.

The following visual shows the multitude of steps that happen automatically and often without our awareness following an incident.

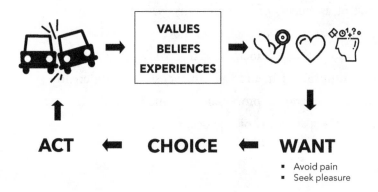

How does this relate to critical conversations?

I was sitting down for a session with Miguel as he started to complain about a coworker, Rabia, who kept interrupting him with urgent issues she needed his expertise in solving. The problem was that most of these issues weren't urgent at all and could easily be solved by Rabia on her own or by a simple Google search. Instead of addressing the issue directly, Miguel stewed in his frustration at Rabia. He wasn't conscious of it, but his desire to avoid the pain of having a critical conversation led him to make a choice. His choice was avoidance. Instead of addressing the issue head on, Miguel let it stew, with each new incident building his frustration, eventually leading to a blowup and a fracture of his working relationship with Rabia.

When a conflict happens, it's extremely difficult to see it objectively. We see it through our own filter, with our biases and expectations wrapped into the situation. We tend to connect what we see and hear to what we already know, our past experiences, and our deep-rooted values and beliefs. We then act in order to protect ourselves from pain or to seek pleasure in the moment, which often goes against the long-term outcome we are looking to achieve. This lack of awareness of how and why we act is our blind spot. Not being aware holds us back from moving forward and making effective progress as a leader. Now that you're aware of it, you can do something about it, and you can choose to act differently. Once we see the filter and the process and become aware of our blind spot, we create the space for choice to occur.

THE STEPS OF HAVING A CRITICAL CONVERSATION

Some years ago, I read the book *Nonviolent Communication*, which forever changed the way I look at and communicate with others. In the 1960s, Dr. Marshall Rosenberg developed a method of communication and conflict resolution called *nonviolent communication*. What drew me to it was its belief that all humans are inherently good, but we resort to harmful behavior as a means to meet our needs as humans, often to seek pleasure or avoid pain. Dr. Rosenberg offered this form of communication as a tool to help resolve conflicts between coworkers, parents, couples, political leaders, and even opposing nations at war.[1]

The nine-step model we'll go through together was born out of this idea. If we can express our needs more clearly and seek to understand others, we'll be better equipped to resolve conflict and drive productive outcomes. The steps are designed to help you avoid your blind spot by bringing an awareness of yourself, your needs, and the situation to the forefront so you can focus on having critical conversations more often, more efficiently, and more effectively. As we go through the steps, use the critical conversation you identified earlier as your example to follow along with. Let's dive into it together.

Part 1: Take a step back

In order to avoid our natural reactions and to compensate for our filter, critical conversations require some emotional distance. Taking a step back allows us to avoid the fight-or-flight response and to focus on what really matters: open, honest, and direct communication. In order to do this, you'll need to first articulate why you need the critical conversation: What outcome do you need it to achieve? You'll need to keep the conversation in the realm of fact, not emotion. You'll have to control your own reactions to keep the conversation on track. Finally, you'll need to commit to your values—and stand by that commitment.

The first part of the nine steps is all about you. It's about assessing the situation, focusing your awareness, and preparing yourself to have the conversation. You'll notice each step in this part is focused inward and often serves as a checklist of sorts. If, after going through these steps, you find you don't have a strong answer to one or more of them, it might be because the conversation you thought was critical is actually not critical and simply requires delivering direct feedback. There may even be no feedback to give at all; you might discover that the situation stemmed from the stories you created and not the person in question.

Step 1: Identify the purpose

Often, we think we need to have a conversation with someone else but don't have a clear desired outcome of the conversation. We really just want to be heard. A critical conversation is not simply about having your side heard; it's about altering the dynamic of a relationship or making a change that impacts your performance, the performance of another, your business, or all of the above. Achieving this goal requires clarity about the outcome you're aiming to get from the conversation.

Looking back to my heated argument with Kevin, it was clear that what I wanted to get out of the critical conversation was a way for us to better communicate disagreements with each other.

ACTIVITY: IDENTIFY THE PURPOSE

- Document the purpose of the conversation you need to have.
- What are you hoping will be different as a result of having the conversation?

It is crucial to be clear about what you are looking to get out of the conversation—to give the other person clarity on the discussion from the start. It helps you avoid blindsiding them and provides you a clear path for the conversation.

Step 2: Focus on the facts

Your conversation should be based strictly on facts—only the information you can gather through observation. Think about it as if a hidden camera captured the event. What does the camera see or hear?

This step is hard. We tend to add in our evaluations to create a story around an event. These stories are often created from our past experiences with the person or of a similar event, and they create a bias around the situation. Each story and inference we make about the situation comes from *our* filter and view of the world. Although it may feel like truth to us, it's our personal, biased assessment of the truth.

Three things usually happen when we judge: The other person gets defensive, they shut down and disengage, or they go on the offensive. None of these outcomes supports moving the conversation forward. Even if your assessment is correct, a critical conversation is not about proving yourself right; it's about getting to a better outcome.

Focusing on the facts requires us to let go of our assessment and look only at the facts—what actually happened, devoid of personal judgments. It's hard to detach our assessment of the truth from the truth itself. That's why taking the time to step back and focus on the facts is so important.

With Kevin, I had a lot of stories I'd built up about him in my head. I believed he didn't care about the business as much as he cared about being right. I didn't think he respected me as a leader, and he thought I was too young and arrogant to be in my role. He didn't think I had what it took to lead the team, and so he shut down all of my ideas, good and bad, before he could even hear them—shutting down disagreements right at the start.

But when I looked back at the incident as if I were watching it recorded by a hidden camera, I didn't see any of that. I actually saw very little. I saw Kevin raise his voice and ask me if I cared about the business and then leave the room. That was it. Those were the facts; the rest was my reaction to it.

ACTIVITY: FOCUS ON THE FACTS

- Document the facts of your situation—and only the facts.
- What would the hidden camera see or hear?

Although there are many evaluations that seem to us to be obvious facts, it's important to remember that we each have our own filter of the world and our own definitions of annoyance, integrity, the right way to do things, and beliefs of right and wrong. When we focus on the facts, we are better able to remove judgment from the situation and then focus clearly on what happened and how to resolve it.

Step 3: Own your reactions

When an inciting incident happens, you have an initial reaction in three ways. There is a *physical reaction*, a rush of *emotion* or several emotions, and an *intellectual reaction* (a set of thoughts).

When Kevin yelled at me, questioned me, and left the room, I thought he was being shortsighted and didn't respect or value my opinion. I got mad, clenched my fists, and felt the muscles in my neck stiffen.

ACTIVITY: OWN YOUR REACTIONS

- Go back to your situation, replay the inciting incident in your mind, and notice how it felt.
- What thought(s) crossed your mind?
- What emotions came over you?
- How did it feel in your body? Did the muscles in your neck tense, or was it a pain in your stomach?

By understanding your reaction, you can then own it. By noticing all the areas in which you react—by noticing your physical body, your emotions, and your thoughts—you open yourself to being aware. You break down your blind spot. You give yourself the space to choose a different response.

Viktor Frankl was a world-famous neurologist and psychiatrist before World War II broke out. As a Jew, he was stripped of his ability to continue his work and lost his job. Although he had an opportunity to flee to the United States to continue his work, he instead chose to remain in Austria. He just couldn't leave his parents behind.

As the war continued, the danger for the Jewish people intensified. Viktor, his wife, Tilly, and parents were deported to the Theresienstadt ghetto, where he lost his father to starvation due to the desperate living conditions. From there, Viktor and his family were shipped on cattle cars to the Auschwitz death camp, where he would eventually lose his brother, mother, and wife.

Viktor lost seemingly everything important in his life—his home, his work, his family, and his freedom. As a psychiatrist, he started to look at the human condition in these death camps, at this profound experience, with a humanistic curiosity. He explored existentially why some people in the camps died and others survived. He could tell which of his friends would not wake up in the morning and which ones would persist despite the gloom ahead of them. He noted his findings in his book *Man's Search for Meaning*, where he shared, "He who has a *why* to live for can bear almost any *how*."[2] The people who held on to a purpose, a reason for life, who could find meaning in getting up in the morning, were more likely to get up and push on.

What Viktor realized was that, however difficult the situation, however hard the Nazis worked to strip him of his dignity, energy, and life, they could not take his mind, his thoughts, and his *why*. These were under his control. In his book, Viktor determined that "everything can be taken from a man but one thing: the last of human freedoms—to choose one's attitude in any given set of circumstances, to choose one's own way." Viktor chose to focus on what he could control rather than what he couldn't. He tapped into the meaning in his life and made a choice to survive and persevere.

I share this story to highlight how, even in life's worst imaginable circumstances, there is still choice. Focusing on what is within your control empowers you.

You might look at your situation and think, *I have a right to be mad*. And you do. The point of owning your feelings is not to dismiss them or deny that an event had an effect on you. Your needs are real, and the event sparked a real feeling. However, as soon as we begin to believe others ultimately have the power to control how we feel and whether our needs are met, we become the victim. If we take responsibility for our feelings and thoughts, we have the power to feel better by seeking ways to get our needs met. If you don't see yourself as part of the problem, you can't be part of the solution. Even in the worst possible situation, Viktor focused on what he could control.

Others may be the stimulus for your behavior, but they are not the cause. Believing that puts others in control of your actions, and you become a victim in your own life. Stop playing the role of the victim; start owning your reactions. Once you decide, once you make the conscious choice to no longer be the victim, to own your reactions, you create an opening to a more productive conversation and better outcomes.

Step 4: Stand in your commitment

What are you committed to as a leader? What is the bigger impact you are looking to have? Instead of focusing on what you don't want to happen anymore, committing to your values and goals as a leader serves as a path to productive action.

My commitment as a leader and in life is to help people unlock their potential. It's what I stand for. As I mentioned earlier, I use this as my North Star, my guiding light to help me approach any critical conversation from this place of helping others rather than of getting what I want or being right.

The focus of this step is setting the intention for the conversation. Even if you don't share the intention with anyone else, it will be felt. By aligning your intention for the conversation with your commitment as a leader, you give yourself a powerful purpose—a *why* with which to approach the conversation from a place of productivity.

ACTIVITY: STAND IN YOUR COMMITMENT

- What is your commitment as a leader?
- Are you upholding that commitment in this conversation?

Up until now, we've really just been having a conversation with ourselves. The point of the two-part process is to force us to take a step back, to give more space between incident and response. Doing so will make it easier for us to choose the most effective response, giving us the highest likelihood of success in the conversation.

Before you jump into having a critical conversation, make sure to step back. In doing this work with leaders, I've noticed the conversation breaks down when you skip a step, when you're convinced you know what you want to say, but you've not focused on the facts or thought it necessary to own your reactions. In taking a shortcut, you shortchange your self-awareness and often miss the root cause of the conversation.

Part 2: Have the conversation

Let's assume you've taken the time to step back, reflected on the purpose of the conversation, focused on the facts, owned your reactions, and taken a stand in your commitment to others. Now it's time to have the conversation. This part of the critical conversation process is much more tactical. As I share the steps with you, I'll continue to prompt you through application activities to prepare the conversation you're looking to have while also giving practical best bets of what to include and what to avoid.

Step 5: Give a heads-up

The first action in having the conversation is pretty simple yet all too often gets botched. The delivery of this step is vital, because it sets the stage for the conversation to come. The action here is simple: Let the other person know you want to have a conversation.

Not only is it a common courtesy to give a heads-up, but it also helps set the expectation for the other person that you're going to be having a conversation on a particular topic. Your intuition might tell you to just spring the conversation on them; after all, you've done the prep and are ready to talk. Avoid this instinct.

Done well, giving a heads-up can allow the other person to feel ready, comfortable, and open to having a conversation with you. Done poorly, it can lead the other person to come into the conversation already on the defensive, with their mind closed to your ideas and feedback, and potentially angry or scared.

A good heads-up is simple. Ask the other person for time to talk, and indicate the purpose of the conversation.

If I'd had this model back then, I'd have shared the heads-up like this: "Kevin, I'd like to connect with you for thirty minutes today or tomorrow about how we can improve the way we communicate disagreements with each other."

Here are some best bets of what to do and what to avoid when giving a heads-up:

DON'T ASK FOR JUST A FEW MINUTES; ASK FOR THIRTY OR MORE

Avoid downplaying the conversation by asking for just a few minutes. There's no way you can hold a critical conversation in just a few minutes. Sure, you can give feedback in a few minutes, but this is a conversation where the other person is going to need time to share their perspective as well. By asking for just a few minutes, you set the conversation up for failure by creating an expectation that it will be quick and simple. Make sure there is sufficient time for the conversation to happen.

DO IT LIVE

Do not attempt to have a critical conversation via chat, text, or email. Ideally, have the conversation in person or via video chat, with phone being the last option. Make sure you're using a communication medium where you can observe the nonverbal cues of the other person and where you can have a real-time dialogue back and forth.

DO NOT THROW A CRITICAL CONVERSATION MEETING ON THEIR CALENDAR

Don't just put it on their calendar. This puts you in a position of power by controlling their schedule and puts them on the defensive. Instead, ask if you can find a time together.

SHARE THE PURPOSE AND NO MORE

When giving a heads-up, don't share the details of what you want to talk about. Taken out of proper context, these details can cause more confusion and defensiveness. Instead of sharing too much, keep it concise and focused. What is the purpose of the conversation—to improve your working relationship, to make a bigger impact on client delivery, to help them take the next step in their leadership? The purpose is high level enough to give them context and broad enough to assuage the defensiveness that comes with asking for these types of conversations.

BE READY TO HAVE THE CONVERSATION NOW

You'll find that people don't like the idea of a critical conversation hanging over their heads. I certainly don't. It gets my mind spinning, and the more time between getting a heads-up and having the conversation, the more stories I create in my head of what the conversation is about and what it means and what the other person thinks of me. Because you're only sharing a snippet of what the conversation is about, the other person will likely want to have the conversation as soon as possible. Make sure you have thirty minutes to connect that day or the following.

Here's what *not* to do: "Hi, Kevin. I want to talk about how we can improve the way we communicate disagreements with each other. I'm out of town the next two weeks, so let's find a time when I get back."

To do this step properly, you'll need to complete and write down the upcoming steps 6 and 7 before you actually give the heads-up. That way, you're prepared and ready to have the conversation before you notify the other person. The setup makes a difference. It impacts the way you and your colleague prepare for and think about the upcoming conversation.

Step 6: Share what didn't work and its impact on you

Imagine you've completed steps 1–5 and you're now in the room with the other person. How do you get started? Start by sharing what didn't work. Be open, honest, and direct. You've already clarified this for yourself by identifying the facts of the situation. The way to think about this step is to focus on the root cause—what didn't work.

While walking a group of leaders through these steps in one of my leadership bootcamps, Ricky, a leader of a tech team, raised her hand and asked, "How many things should I share? I've got three critical things Shaun missed that I need to discuss with him." Ricky's question was valid. When we think about finally having the critical conversation, a natural tendency is to pile on all the things we want this person to do differently. Why have multiple different conversations? Let's just rip the Band-Aid off all at once, right? Wrong. Think about the last time a family member berated you on something you didn't do to their liking. Then, in the middle of the conversation, they started to add more and more things you don't do well. How does that feel? Does it make you more likely to take action on any of your shortcomings? Probably not.

I told Ricky what I'll tell you: Pick one—only one. First, start by asking yourself, *What's at the root of this behavior?* Which one fact from the many you've captured, if changed, would make the biggest impact and transition toward the outcome you're trying to achieve?

This step is hard, because it requires us to focus on what we really want out of the conversation. You might have thought you knew the behavior you wanted to see changed, but only when you have put words to just one item are you ready to share it with the other person. How can you expect them to change if you're not clear on what action of theirs didn't work?

Once you are clear on what didn't work, you then have an opportunity to share the impact the incident had on you or the business. Try to avoid speaking for others about how this person's behavior impacted them. Rather, share what didn't work and its impact on you. Your colleague can't deny those effects, and it adds a bit more weight to why you are sitting down in the first place.

Example:

Restate the purpose

"Kevin, I wanted to sit down because I'm concerned about how we communicate disagreements with each other. I'd like to share my perspective, hear yours, and have a conversation about how we can improve the way we communicate."

Share what didn't work

"During our account review meeting last week, after I shared an idea for how to solve ABC Corp.'s complaint, I noticed you ended the conversation by leaving the room."

And its impact

"It stopped our meeting in its tracks. We weren't able to come to a solution for how to approach ABC Corp. I fear our inability to communicate disagreements with each other will hold us back from serving our clients' needs and succeeding as a business."

ACTIVITY: THE ROOT CAUSE

- Restate the purpose of the conversation.
- Write down what didn't work.
  - Look back at your facts section, and pick the action the other person did that didn't work. It is OK to share a few actions that highlight the main action.
  - For example, "Kevin left the room" highlights the main action of him shutting down the conversation after I shared a different idea.
- Document the impact of the main action.

Although there may be many things you want to address, pick only one, the one that if addressed will make the biggest impact on the desired outcome you'd like to achieve. When you focus on this one, you make it easier for the other person to take in the feedback and improve your odds of reaching a successful outcome together.

Step 7: Make a request

When you make the request for change, it's up to you to be clear about what you want the other person to do differently. It's one thing to share what didn't work and the impact; the next thing to do is obvious but important not to miss. Make your request of the other person.

Example:

Restate the purpose

"Kevin, I wanted to sit down because I'm concerned about how we communicate disagreements with each other. I'd like to share my perspective, hear yours, and have a conversation about how we can improve the way we communicate."

Share what didn't work

"During our account review meeting last week, after I shared an idea for how to solve ABC Corp.'s complaint, I noticed you ended the conversation by leaving the room."

Its impact

"It stopped our meeting in its tracks. We weren't able to come to a solution for how to approach ABC Corp. I fear our inability to communicate disagreements with each other will hold us back from serving our clients' needs and succeeding as a business."

Make your request

"When we come to a disagreement, I'd like you to ask me for the reasoning behind my opinion."

Here are some best bets for making a request:

MAKE A REQUEST, NOT A DEMAND

If you are having a critical conversation with a direct report, you must still make a request of them. If you expect them to do what you say, then it's simply a demand dressed up as a request. If you're not open to leaving the room with a different outcome than what you've requested, this is not a critical conversation; it's a reprimand, an ultimatum, or just direct feedback. I'm not saying each of these doesn't have a role in the workplace; what I'm saying is that these are not critical conversations.

If you remember from earlier in the chapter, a critical conversation requires both parties to be involved, to share their perspectives, and to work together to reach the optimal solution. By masking a request as a demand, you run the risk of making your colleague feel trapped and possibly tricked, because your words don't match your actions and expectations. Check your intention before you have this conversation. Ensure you're open to having a real conversation and having it go in a direction you can't readily predict.

SAY WHAT YOU WANT—NOT WHAT YOU DON'T WANT

Instead of telling them what you want them to stop doing, take it a step further by offering what you want them to do instead. You'll notice in the previous example, I didn't ask Kevin to stop storming out of the room or to stop shutting down conversations where we disagree. Instead, I asked him to engage me by asking questions, which would require him to remain in the conversation with me.

BE CLEAR ON THE ACTIONS YOU WANT THEM TO DO—NOT WHO YOU WANT THEM TO BE

We tend to insert our judgments and evaluations of the other person here: Stop being a jerk; stop losing your temper with me; remain cool, calm, and collected when we disagree. But none of these are actions. They are ways of being, which are difficult to change, even if the other person is entirely on board. Instead, share the specific action you want them to take. This provides multiple benefits: It will be easier for the other person to take action and for you to assess whether they are doing it. More specific means easier to measure and assess.

It's easy to look at this step and get tripped up. Where do I start? How do I make sure to use the right language? How can I write out the specific actions? Here's a little secret: You already did the hard work for this step when you focused on the facts and again when you wrote out what didn't work. Making the request is usually as simple as taking what didn't work and turning it into a request of what you want them to do. Try it out now.

ACTIVITY: YOUR REQUEST

- Write down your request now.

When you ask for what you want, when you make it clear and actionable, you increase your chances of getting it. So be clear here.

Step 8: Create an opening for possibility

Creating an opening for possibility is the most missed or misused step in the process. It's the difference between the request being a demand or an ultimatum and it being part of a critical conversation. Making a request does not lead to the outcome of the conversation; it's actually just the start. Steps 6 and 7 only take up the first few minutes of the critical conversation. The bulk of the conversation sits here, in creating an opening for possibility. This is where you actually have to be open to the idea that the other person's perspective might change your outcome, open to how they see the situation. Being open to possibility requires you to listen to the other person with intention and attention and to ask powerful questions as they share. It requires you to use the skills you've already built up in chapters 4 and 5.

To give you a better frame of reference for how to hold the conversation, here's a tool you can use to plan out and prepare for your upcoming critical conversation.

ACTIVITY: DIAGRAMMING THE DISCUSSION

This diagram should give you a better picture of how important creating an opening is.

5 minutes	Share what didn't work, its impact and your request
20 minutes	Create an opening for possibility
5 minutes	Align on next steps

This step is where the conversation really happens, as you can see from the diagram. Although you've spent a considerable amount of time preparing for the conversation, taken a step back, thought about the purpose, and communicated your request, all of those steps are designed to allow you now just to be in the conversation with the other person, to be open to the possibilities that come from listening and asking. Once you share your request, shut up and listen.

With Kevin, it was time to get out of my head and listen to his side of the story, to hear his perspective. In listening to Kevin, I began to see the situation differently, to empathize the line he was balancing between making our client happy and making sure we provide the best product to them. Though he could see how some of the suggested changes hindered our operational effectiveness, he was more worried that by not making the changes, we could lose the client. By creating an opening for possibility, Kevin and I were better able to understand each other and align on a common goal, setting our business up to succeed in the long term.

The power of being open is best highlighted in the story of C. P. Ellis and Ann Atwater. It takes place in the middle of the civil rights movement in the 1970s in America. At the time, C. P. Ellis was the president of the Durham, North Carolina, Ku Klux Klan chapter and was forced into working alongside Ann Atwater, a black female civil rights activist, when they were named co-chairs of a school board project to plan how to desegregate the Durham public schools. They obviously had very different opinions about how and to what level this should happen for the students. They came from different backgrounds, had vastly different perspectives on the world, and were now paired together to come up with the best possible solution for the students of Durham.

Instead of trying to convince Ellis of her position, Atwater started by listening and being open. After ten days of meetings together, an unexpected transformation occurred: Ellis resigned from the KKK and took up as a civil rights activist.

When asked to share what had happened, Ellis said, "I used to think that Ann Atwater was the meanest black woman I'd ever seen in my life . . . But, you know, her and I got together one day for an hour or two and talked. And she is trying to help her people like I'm trying to help my people."[3]

In feeling more connected to Atwater, Ellis realized he could no longer hold his racist beliefs and renounced his membership in the Klan. All Atwater did was create an opening for possibility. She listened, found common ground, and was open to a possibility that no one could have imagined ten days prior. The impact of this step can be profound.

Step 9: Align on the next steps

Since we each have our own filter, our own unique way in which we see, hear, and experience the world, it's fairly easy to misunderstand each other in conversation. What you thought you agreed to in your discussion may be misinterpreted or could have been ill defined; a week later, you may find yourself facing the same issues as before. This happens when you fail to clearly align on the next steps.

It's this last step, the one that's actually the easiest and simplest to complete, that we must not skip. If you've created a true opening for possibility, the outcome from this step will probably be a bit different from the request you made while still driving toward your desired outcome, meeting the purpose of the conversation.

The best way to make sure you're aligned is, prior to leaving the meeting, to recap the actions each of you will take in the coming days. Don't leave the room without ensuring confirmation on next steps. Sometimes that may mean the next steps are to schedule more time to continue the conversation if you've not been able to finish it properly. Then follow up with an email asking for confirmation of the agreed-upon action steps.

Example

"Kevin, thank you for taking the time to sit down and talk about how we can improve the way we communicate with each other.

"Here's what I heard as next steps from the conversation. Please review and let me know if you heard the same. When we come to a disagreement, one that is heated, that ends up with us ending the meeting:

- "I agree to allow you space to think and remind myself that you are frustrated with the situation, not with me.

- "You agree to come back to me within twenty-four hours to meet again and determine the best next steps together.

"Is this what you heard too? If not, let's reconnect and realign on our actions."

As you can see from my example above, the actions we each took in the end were different from the request I'd initially made, yet they still achieved my desired outcome of planning for how we can better communicate with each other. Taking this extra step helps give you both assurance that you've properly heard each other and are aligned on where to go next. It also gives you something to reference when holding the other person accountable to their behaviors and actions.

You're now done. From this point on, it's about what you do next, how you follow up and hold up your end of the bargain; otherwise this conversation won't have the impact you'd hoped for. The conversation won't mean anything if you don't follow through on your agreed-upon actions and hold the other person accountable to theirs. People will do what you do, not what you say. By deeming this conversation critical, there is something at stake, so make sure you continue the work you've put in by being open, honest, and direct in your follow-up and follow-through.

SCRIPT FOR HOLDING A CRITICAL CONVERSATION

STEP 1: IDENTIFY THE PURPOSE

What are you hoping will be different as a result of having the conversation?

- I want us to be better at communicating disagreements with each other.

STEP 2: FOCUS ON THE FACTS

What would the hidden camera see or hear?

- Kevin raised his voice and asked me if I cared about the business and then left the room.

STEP 3: OWN YOUR REACTIONS

Go back to your situation, replay the inciting incident in your mind, and notice how it felt.

What thought crossed your mind?

- I thought he was being shortsighted and didn't respect or value my opinion.

What emotions came over you?

- Anger, fear, and doubt.

How did it feel in your body? Did the muscles in your neck tense, or was it a pain in your stomach?

- I clenched my fists and felt the muscles in my neck stiffen.

STEP 4: STAND IN YOUR COMMITMENT

What is your commitment as a leader? Are you upholding that commitment in this conversation?

- I want to help us unlock the potential of our business and thus of our working together.

STEP 5: GIVE A HEADS-UP

- "Kevin, I wanted to sit down because I'm concerned about how we communicate disagreements with each other. I'd like to share my perspective, hear yours, and have a conversation about how we can improve the way we communicate."

STEP 6: SHARE WHAT DIDN'T WORK
AND ITS IMPACT ON YOU

- "During our account review meeting last week, after I shared an idea for how to solve ABC Corp.'s complaint, I noticed you ended the conversation by leaving the room."

- "It stopped our meeting in its tracks. We weren't able to come to a solution for how to approach ABC Corp. I fear our inability to communicate disagreements with each other will hold us back from serving our clients' needs and succeeding as a business."

continued

STEP 7: MAKE A REQUEST

- "When we come to a disagreement, I'd like you to ask me for the reasoning behind my opinion."

STEP 8: CREATE AN OPENING FOR POSSIBILITY

- "I had to shut up and listen to Kevin's side of the story."

STEP 9: ALIGN ON THE NEXT STEPS

Get clear on your next steps in the meeting and follow up with an email.

Kevin, thank you for taking the time to sit down and talk about how we can improve the way we communicate with each other.

Here's what I heard as next steps from the conversation; please review and let me know if you heard the same. When we come to a disagreement, one that is heated, that ends up with us ending the meeting, this is what I understand:

- I agree to allow you space to think and remind myself that you are frustrated with the situation, not with me.
- You agree to come back to me within twenty-four hours to meet again and determine the best next steps together.

Is this what you heard too? If not, let's reconnect and realign on our actions.

Cheers,
Aaron

WHAT'S THE POINT?

There is an art to holding a critical conversation in a way the other person feels heard, and you both move forward together. It won't be comfortable the first time around, and you likely won't be great at it, either. Like all of the other skills we've been working on together, they take practice. The more you hold these conversations, the better you'll get at delivering the feedback. I can't say they will get easier. They are conversations with people. Giving critical feedback will continue to be hard until you realize that feedback is a gift and that by not giving this feedback, you are robbing people of an opportunity to grow.

In providing you with these steps, my goal is to make it easier for you to prepare yourself to hold a productive critical conversation, and yet the feedback I receive most often from leaders when reflecting on this process is the importance of having the conversation sooner rather than later. It's natural to want to put off the conversation, to tell yourself it's not that important or you're too busy. It's natural to want to avoid the pain and discomfort of confronting a person. In assessing the critical nature of the conversation through the critical conversation checklist, realize there is something more important than your discomfort, that there's a better outcome on the other end. Holding a critical conversation can mean embracing the short-term discomfort while knowing there is something more important on the other side of the conversation.

Go out, be courageous, and give the gift of feedback to your team. It will make you and everyone around you better.

TOP TAKEAWAYS

- The more you hold back on sharing feedback and the more protection you give your employee, the more you rob them of their growth. Whether they acknowledge your honesty in the moment or five years later or never, by sharing the harsh truths, you allow someone else the opportunity to learn and to grow.

- A critical conversation requires a critique or change to a behavior that is crucial to the way you work and the success of your team or business.

- We rarely notice the impact of not having a critical conversation immediately, although the repercussions of avoiding it can haunt us for weeks, months, or years.

- Although you can't guarantee the outcome of a conversation, you can set yourself up to achieve the best possible outcome.

- We each have our filter through which we see the world. Our filters are made up of our values, our beliefs of right and wrong, what we expect from others, and all of our past experiences. Your filter impacts the way you see and experience the world around you.

- Humans have two desires that can explain most human behaviors: the desire to avoid pain and the desire to seek pleasure.

- The nine-step process is designed to bring an awareness of yourself, your needs, and the situation to the forefront so you can focus on having critical conversations more often, more efficiently, and more effectively.

- Part 1 is all about you. It's about assessing the situation, focusing your awareness, and preparing yourself to have the conversation.

- Part 2 is much more tactical, prompting you to get clear on how you want to communicate this issue to another person.

- Your critical conversation shouldn't end once the conversation ends. It should live on in the actions you and the other person take as a result of the conversation.

- Most of all, don't forget: Feedback is a gift!

ACTION ITEMS

- Pick one critical conversation you need to have, walk through all nine steps of the process to prepare, and then hold one critical conversation with an employee, colleague, or boss.

REFLECTION

- What was the outcome of your critical conversation? What worked? What didn't?

- What did you learn that you can apply going forward?

- What will you do differently in holding your next critical conversation?

PART 3

PUTTING IT ALL TOGETHER

In Part 3, we're going to take everything we've learned so far and begin to piece it all together into a road map for bringing open, honest, and direct leadership to your team. We'll outline ways to make sure you're getting the most out of each meeting with your team and walk through the steps so you can get started today by organizing and scheduling leadership into your current routine.

As you dive into this last section, I want to share again my goal in writing this book: for you to be able to put one idea into consistent action. Small changes taken consistently over time lead to profound impact. Let's put the plan together to make the small changes happen.

Chapter 8

STEPS TO MOVE FORWARD

*"At every step and every juncture in life,
there is the opportunity to learn."*

—Ryan Holiday, author, entrepreneur

Intention: Being open, honest, and direct makes you and
your team stronger.

Before founding Raise The Bar, I served as the head of operations and education for a health and well-being startup. An essential trait of our leadership team was holding information about our financial status close to our chest. At the time, the rationale made sense: We didn't want our coaches and team members to worry about their jobs. Yes, we were a startup, but we wanted to give our team a sense of stability so they could keep excelling and not have to worry about the business aspect.

Then one day, we had to let go of 15% of our team. It wasn't out of the blue, though. A year prior, we'd made a bet. We bet our sales would continue to grow, and extra team members would not only help us deliver our increased demand for coaching in the short term but also provide the capacity to expand to future clients. I convinced our founders of this need based on my analysis, and I was wrong. My forecasting failure is one of the toughest lessons I've experienced, because being wrong directly impacted people's lives.

We knew once we made the layoffs official that we couldn't go back to business as usual. We had to give our team an explanation. Even writing this, I can still feel the tightness in my stomach from the fear and anxiety I held leading up to this meeting. Our COO encouraged all of us to stop making excuses and simply be open, honest, and direct.

So that's what we did. We laid out the entire financial situation for the team. We told them for the first time in four years that we didn't know if we'd make it through the year. We shared how we had a narrow runway, and if we executed on a few key initiatives, we could be successful. I gave in to my vulnerability, let go of the tightness, and I won't forget that day and the energy in the room. The people I was afraid would run for the hills at the uncertainty stood up and said they were all in. The energy shifted from fear to possibility. The team was ready to make this business work and step up in any way they could.

In the subsequent months, our people asked me what else they could do, how they could help secure new business or give a free coaching session to a prospective client. I noticed team members from other departments coming together to work on projects and do the extra work that was needed.

In sharing our vulnerability with the team, we not only showed them we were fallible but also allowed them to truly feel like owners of the company, not just employees. The lesson from this experience was clear to me: Being open, honest, and direct—something we thought would scare our team away—brought us together.

Many founders and CEOs I work with are afraid of being this exposed. It's scary. You're vulnerable. You're admitting you don't have all the answers. Being open, honest, and direct is about saying, "I don't know the right answer, and I don't know if everything is going to be all right."

In a study, Elliot Aronson, Ben Willerman, and Joanne Floyd tested the impact making a mistake had on a leader's likeability.[1] It turns out that highly competent people who made a mistake ended up being more likeable than before. This is better known in social psychology as the *pratfall effect*. It flies in the face of the picture of a traditional stoic leader who has all the answers, never makes mistakes, and always knows which way to go. No one has all the answers, though; no one person is always right. When you allow yourself to let go of control, you give your people the chance to opt in, as well as show them that you, too, make mistakes and are human. When they see this, they dive all in because they feel more connected to your company and its purpose and to you as their leader. There is a perspective shift: They go from seeing it as a job to being deeply committed to the company's vision.

Instead of shielding your team from the responsibility of making the company a success, be honest with them, and allow them to see and feel what that means. Allow them to be a part of the success alongside you.

Before your next all-hands meeting, ask yourself these three questions:

- What am I trying to protect my team from?
- What am I not sharing as a result?
- What's the impact of withholding this information on me, the team, and the company?

Instead of withholding information, allow yourself to be open, honest, and direct about your biggest concerns and struggles. It will help your people feel more connected to you and more invested in the company. If you want your people to go all in—if you want to get the most out of them—start sharing what *all in* really means by doing it yourself. Start by being authentic, by sharing your wins and losses, and by sharing your company with them.

SCHEDULING YOUR LEADERSHIP

Depending on how many direct reports you have, roughly 30% of the time will be spent on leading your people, whether it's through one-on-one meetings, team meetings, dealing with fires, training, or assessing your people. That's almost two full days a week!

You might be saying to yourself that you don't take that amount of time or don't need that amount of time with your people. Or you might think your business structure doesn't support spending that amount of time on management. But it's not really a choice. This time will be spent, regardless of whether you want to or not.

The question becomes how and when you want to spend that time. If you decide to not plan time to hold one-on-one meetings with your people, if you don't take the time to listen to them and help them evaluate their work, you will save time up front; but time won't be saved in the long run. The time saved not engaging with your employees will show up later when you'll have to drop everything because your employee didn't understand the expectations of the project. It might come when an employee hands you her two-week's notice and you have to put everything on hold to create a role description, interview candidates, and get someone new up to speed.

The alternative is much preferable in my mind. You can choose to schedule the time you're going to spend leading. You can be proactive and strategic about it. Here are a few suggested meetings to put on your calendar now to get ahead of these issues and lead with intention.

The one-on-one meeting

Also known as a check-in meeting, the one-on-one is most effective when done consistently with each employee. It might be every week for some who need more attention or every two weeks for others. The recommendation here is to have some sort of consistent touchpoint with your employee every few weeks. The one-on-one is your chance to help your employee troubleshoot weekly tasks while also realigning priorities. The purpose is to hold her accountable and give any insights needed to do her best.

Conversations like this give insight into the progress of your team and help you recalibrate among the busyness of the week. It affords your employees the opportunity to get help on specific issues while also making sure their energies are spent on the most pressing business needs.

Use the agenda outline below as a launching point.

- **Updates:** Here is a chance for both of you to share any relevant updates, to review goals and actions taken from the last check-in.

- **Working items:** This is the time to help her with issues from the past week.

- **Action items:** End the meeting aligning on next steps for each of you; recapping this in an email is an effective way to hold both of you accountable.

The one-on-one meeting can happen anywhere—in person, over the phone—but plan for fifteen to thirty minutes. It shouldn't take much longer, since you're meeting regularly. Before meeting, spend a few minutes reviewing last week's action items, add relevant notes for the current meeting, and ask your employee to do the same.

The stay interview

Scheduling your leadership also means you consistently hold stay interviews with each of your employees. These are quarterly conversations with your employee about how they want to grow, how they want to develop, and how you can help them get there. The purpose of this conversation is to connect with your employee, show them you care, and learn how you can support their development. Remember, stay interviews should happen outside of a typical meeting—maybe over lunch or coffee or on a walk. Taking this time with your employees shows them you care about their future while creating an opportunity for you to be a coach in their growth.

I recommend going back to chapter 4 (page 69) or to the leadership toolkit (page 196) to see the steps. Plan for about thirty to sixty minutes for each stay interview.

The performance conversation

Make sure to hold a performance conversation—ideally quarterly or biannually. If your company requires doing them only once a year, that doesn't mean you can't have them more often. The purpose of this meeting is to evaluate the performance of your employee and to understand how she is tracking toward her long-term goals—measuring how she compared with her quarterly targets. This conversation is a time to assess her growth toward current goals and to set future goals.

Have your employee come to the meeting prepared to share her results. It's often best to review these before the meeting. The performance conversation is a powerful way to look at the big picture for your employee—pulling out of the weekly working items—giving her objective feedback on her growth and goals.

Here are a few sample questions I ask my team:

- What are some significant accomplishments from last quarter?

- What didn't go as planned? What happened? What did you learn?

- What is an area of growth you want to focus on for next quarter?

- What can I do to better support you?

Plan for between sixty and ninety minutes for each review, with at least thirty minutes of prep time ahead of the meeting.

The self check-in

The most successful leaders make time not only for their team but also for themselves. It's so easy to get caught up in the day to day, going from one meeting to another and seemingly not having time to pick your head up and take a strategic look forward.

This weekly check-in with yourself is where you take the time to reflect on the week that just passed, to look forward to next week's lineup of meetings, and to plan strategically what you need to accomplish versus what you have time to accomplish. I suggest setting aside an hour every Friday afternoon or Monday morning on your calendar to make sure you set up yourself and your week for success.

Here are three steps to follow when conducting your weekly self-reflection:

Reflect on the past week

Take a look at your calendar, your to-do list, and your goals to clarify what you accomplished, what you missed, what you did well, and what you're proud of. This step is designed to help you identify gaps and celebrate successes.

Plan the week ahead

Look at your calendar for next week. What do you have coming up? What prep work do you need to do? What big projects and small tasks do you need to accomplish by the end of the week? Use these questions to make your to-do list. If you don't have enough time to do everything on the list, look to the next paragraph.

Say no, delegate, or delay

Based on the meetings you already have on your calendar, your personal or family commitments, and the projects you need to make progress on in the coming week, you've likely planned more work than you have time to accomplish. Instead of telling yourself you can get it all done, be a bit more realistic and strategic. Use these four questions to determine what you are really going to get done in the week.

- What takes priority?
- What should you be saying no to?
- What can you delegate to someone else?
- What do you have to delay?

Once you've worked through these questions, you should have a more clearly defined plan of meetings, projects, and tasks. You're now set up for success in the next week.

If you take the few minutes today to put each of these on the calendar, you'll stop worrying about being there for your people because you've already set aside time to listen, ask, and support them on a weekly, monthly, and annual basis. Scheduling your leadership drives consistency in the way you lead, what you accomplish, and what others can expect of you as a leader. When you do this, you create a whole lot more clarity for yourself and your employees. It will give you focus while also empowering your people to own their growth.

DO ONE THING WELL

I know there is a lot of information in this book, a lot of ideas that may spark you to take action, a lot that you want to make sure you incorporate into your leadership toolkit today. I encourage you to take that energy and move it toward taking one action, not ten. Start small. If all you take from this book is one thing, one idea, one action, and you start applying it to the way you lead, you're moving in the right direction.

Write down the one thing you want to focus on, how you're going to make it happen, and how you'll track your progress. Do it now! Focus on consistently taking action toward this focus, on learning from what's working and what's not, and I promise your actions will have an impact.

WHERE WE'VE COME

We've come a long way together. Thank you for your energy, engagement, and hard work. We started on this journey together in part

1, where we discussed why most managers suck and how to get it right when hiring and promoting managers in your company. We looked at the traits that define great leaders and dug down to find the underlying skills practiced and actions taken by great leaders. We looked at the critical difference between knowing what to do and actually doing it in chapter 3. Remember the field of grass analogy? We walked through the process of developing a new habit and laid out the steps to make it easier for you to create that new path, the new skill, and repeatedly follow the new path.

We changed gears in part 2, where we focused on learning and applying the skills it takes to be better at leading people. Each chapter served as a practical guide for you and your managers to practice going down the ideal path. We set an intention to develop the skills of your leaders so you can get more out of your people. In chapter 4, we looked at the "bloomers" study, which highlighted the importance of listening with intention and attention. We identified your listening blind spot and introduced the stay interview as a way to practice listening with your team today. In chapter 5, we explored the systematic irrationalities of our brain through confirmation bias and learned how to overcome this blind spot by engaging in our three-year-old self—our curiosity as a means to be better evaluators of people and situations.

Chapter 6 centered on the importance of clarity and psychological safety as key ingredients for creating and sustaining a high-performance team. Without either of these, people don't know what they are working toward, how they should work together (the rules of the game), and how they can hold themselves and others accountable. We created our own team agreements, discussed how to make deals with your team, and then learned a set of tips to model open, honest, and direct communication with your people. We finished with the last and often most difficult skill to practice: critical conversations. This skill requires more than just knowing the steps to take but also a mindset shift, an understanding that as human beings we all see the world through our own filter; and in order to help others grow, we must be willing to give them the critical feedback even if it's uncomfortable in the moment, because feedback is a gift.

The chapters were laid out in a specific order, with each chapter built on your ability to understand and practice the previous chapter's skill. It starts with listening; in order to properly be able to ask powerful questions, you first need to be able to listen with intention and attention. Open, honest, and direct communication doesn't happen if you've not first shown your people you care, you hear them, and you are a strategic leader who constantly digs beneath the surface to evaluate the core issues at hand. You now have the four essential skills to be a better leader of people, to elevate your game from where you started to where you want to go.

WHERE DO YOU GO FROM HERE?

Start by taking the smallest action. Small actions taken consistently over time make a powerful impact. We rarely notice them because as leaders, we are constantly looking forward, forgetting to celebrate our successes along the way. We learn most from our mistakes because we sit in them, try to understand them, and make adjustments to avoid them in the future. As important as this is, it's equally important to celebrate your successes, however small they are, and to take a long look at what worked so you can make sure to continue doing it in the future. When we fail to identify the wins, we easily lose track of what's worked, failing to notice our true factors of success. Don't worry about developing all four skills right away. Start with one action, with one skill, and see the impact that developing it into a consistent practice has on your team.

If you've not yet put the activities into practice, go back to the summary pages at the end of chapters 4–7, review them, and do the activities for each. Take one activity per week, then go back to the chapter summary and use the reflection questions to assess what worked, what didn't, and what needs to be adjusted for the next time you put your learning into practice. Each of the tools in the book can also be found in the leadership toolkit or, in a more interactive way, online at *openhonestanddirect.com*.

WHAT'S THE POINT?

Open, honest, and direct leadership means you are present, ready to listen, curious as an evaluator, direct in your communication, and ready to take the next hard step, even if that means holding a critical conversation.

When you practice these skills consistently over time, you and your leaders start to create a culture of learning, in which everyone is working together to reach the best possible outcome: a culture where you, your leaders, and the entire team get to be themselves and are rewarded for it with fun, fulfillment, and success.

This freedom and growth come from doing the work. What I've shared in this book was designed to trigger you to take action, to help you and your leaders move from knowing what to do to actually doing it. The great secret of leadership isn't the knowledge of what makes a great leader or even what gets in the way of your leadership. It is being willing to take the next hard step, to do the work it takes to lead others, to act with intention and choice and not by circumstance. This requires effort, energy, and commitment from you and your leaders. Change is not easy, but I hope I showed through this book that it's also not too complex.

Even with all the tools and skills learned in this book, to ultimately get the most out of your people, you need to be real, to be yourself, because no tool can replace authenticity, humility, and vulnerability. The best leaders are the ones who know themselves, who are willing to be open, honest, and direct. In doing this, you'll be on the path to getting the most out of your people.

Everything you want, any change you seek, is just outside of your comfort zone. Continue embracing a beginner's mindset, continue challenging your status quo, continue showing up with authenticity and humility, and you will see results.

LEADERSHIP TOOLKIT

I f you're ready to take action and start practicing the skills from this book, I've compiled the activities and key models for you here.

CHAPTER 1: WHY MOST MANAGERS SUCK

Hire right

The most important thing to do is make sure you have the right people in the right seats. This means taking a step back and looking at your hiring and promotion practices for leaders. Before hiring a manager, I recommend first asking yourself these three questions.

ACTIVITY: THREE QUESTIONS FOR HIRING RIGHT

☐ Does she want to lead?

☐ Do I have the right metrics in place to measure her success?

☐ Does she have the skills to lead others?

ACTIVITY: IDENTIFY YOUR INDIVIDUAL CONTRIBUTORS

1. Create a list of all your people managers.

2. Go through each manager on the list one by one and ask yourself:

   a. Does she truly want to lead? (yes, no)

   b. What is the impact of her managing people on your team? (positive, neutral, negative)

   c. Is she better served as an individual contributor? (yes, no)

3. Put a big star by each manager who is a better fit as an individual contributor.

4. Determine your course of action with each manager.

EVALUATING MANAGERS				
Manager name	Do they truly want to lead? (yes, no)	What's the impact of their managing people? (positive, neutral, negative)	Are they better served as an individual contributor? (yes, no)	Action to take
Noel	Yes	Neutral	No	Invest in her development as a leader.
Steve	No	Negative	Yes	Share insights with Steve and opportunity to transition to more strategic role where he doesn't manage people.
Latoya	Yes	Positive	Yes	Check in with her to learn what she's doing well and how you can continue to support her.

CHAPTER 2: WHAT MAKES A LEADER GREAT

Habits of a leader

Instead of spending our time focused solely on the outcomes great leaders produce, we need to put more energy into the actions that drive the outcomes.

CHAPTER 3: HOW HABIT FORMATION WORKS

A process for habit development

The learn-apply-reflect model is designed to get your leaders practicing skills and putting them into action. The quicker and more frequently a leader can take their new skill, apply it to a real-life situation, and dissect their performance of it, the quicker the skill becomes a habit.

CHAPTER 4: LISTEN WITH INTENTION AND ATTENTION

Notice your inner dialogue

We all have internal conversations, but few of us pay attention to them well enough to control them. If you listen first to yourself, you can control your inner monologue so that you can then truly listen to others.

Here's an activity you can use to test yourself on this skill.

ACTIVITY: BEING IN SILENCE

1. Find a partner.

2. Sit directly in front of your partner so that you are facing each other with your knees almost touching.

3. Set a timer on your phone for three minutes and then put your phone facedown, near you, and in silent mode.

4. Stay silent with this other person for the full three minutes.

What thoughts ran through your head during this time? Did you look around the room? How many times did you think about the alarm and hope it would go off? Did you notice how uncomfortable the silence was? This is your inner dialogue. It's where 90% of every conversation occurs—within your brain. Even if you're thinking, *This guy is crazy; I don't have an inner dialogue!* you are engaging with your inner dialogue at this very moment.

Your listening blind spot

We each show up with a tendency we fall back on when listening to others. Some of us listen to connect ideas; some of us listen to solve a problem; others listen to figure out what they are going to say next. Each of us listens *for* something, *to do* something. This is your listening blind spot.

Common listening blind spots are when we listen

- To determine my next steps
- To decide if I should pay attention
- To validate my ideas
- To make sure I'm heard
- To figure out what I'm going to say next
- To prove myself
- To learn the other person's intentions

- To understand the issue

- To make my point

- To help the other person

ACTIVITY: DISCOVER YOUR LISTENING BLIND SPOT

1. What is your natural tendency when listening to others (at work or home)? What are you listening to do?

   You may feel that several of the blind spots listed earlier describe you. For the sake of becoming a better listener, pick one. This is where you will focus your awareness and attention.

   I listen to _____.

2. How has your blind spot helped you in your career?

3. How has it held you back?

4. What impact does your blind spot have on your team?

Checklist for listening

ACTIVITY: CHECKLIST FOR LISTENING

Follow this checklist prior to a conversation in which you know it's important to be present, and to listen with intention and attention.

☐ **Remember your listening blind spot**

Simply being aware of your own listening blind spot ahead of time will help you notice when you are doing it. And when you notice, you can choose to stop.

☐ Remove all distractions

This step is about removing the distractions that will get in the way of you being able to be present in the conversation. It could mean putting your phone on silent, turning off alerts on your computer, or not having your phone out. Even the presence of your phone facedown on the table during a meeting is a distraction for your brain, which is why my phone stays on silent in my pocket!

☐ Clarify the meeting's purpose

Start the meeting by getting clear on the purpose. What is each person trying to accomplish in this meeting? What would success at the end of the meeting look like? By beginning with the end in mind, you can let go of trying to wonder what the point of the meeting is and stay on task with the person and the meeting.

The stay interview

It's time you put your learning into practice by holding a *stay interview*. A stay interview is the opposite of an exit interview. Instead of learning about why the person has decided to leave your company, it's about going upstream and getting clarity on what will make your employee stay with you and your organization. A stay interview helps you connect with an employee outside of a normal one-on-one meeting, to learn about them and their desires for growth. Take the employee to coffee, out for lunch, or even on a walk around the block. Your primary goal is to learn about where your employee sees themselves in the next few years and what they want for their career.

Start by asking these two questions, and then build on what you hear:

1. What skills are you looking to develop?

2. How can I support you?

ACTIVITY: THE STAY INTERVIEW

1. Outside of your normal 1-1
2. Start by asking
   a. What skills are you looking to develop?
   b. How can I support you?
3. Shut up and listen

CHAPTER 5: ASK POWERFUL QUESTIONS

Powerful questions checklist

Here's a checklist to help you determine if the question was powerful or not . . .

ACTIVITY: POWERFUL QUESTIONS CHECKLIST

Is the question

- Open ended?
- Beginner's mindset?
- Clear and succinct?
- In context?
- Impactful?
- In the moment?

The hot seat

ACTIVITY: THE HOT SEAT

The goal of this activity is to provide you and your team a platform to practice asking powerful questions. I especially love this because it forces you and your leaders to ask questions of real work scenarios you are facing today. In addition to helping you practice, it will also help you and your team solve key people-issues you're facing.

Prior to your next team meeting, ask one team member to come prepared to share a challenge they are facing, one to which they don't know the answer. It usually works best when they type up a few notes and share with the team beforehand. Here are a few tips to guide your team member in their preparations.

continued

- The problem: Use one sentence to describe the problem you are looking for help with.

- What's at stake: What makes this problem so important to solve?

- The facts: What are crucial facts to know about the problem? Describe these in three to five bullet points.

- The purpose: What's your desired outcome? What would success look like?

Give the team member two to three minutes to describe the challenge and what success would look like for them in the given situation in the team meeting. Then share the powerful questions checklist so all can see. Go around the room, with each team member firing away a question of the presenter with the goal of learning more about the problem and, ultimately, of helping the presenter achieve their desired outcome. Avoid asking leading questions. Allow around twenty minutes for this.

Close out your questions by asking each person what they learned from this activity.

Hopefully, they—and you—will learn the power of asking questions versus giving advice and the impact it can have on someone's ability to learn, grow, and make impactful change. You'll also begin to notice what a powerful question looks like. Powerful questions are not formulaic, even when you have a checklist to follow. You can't simply write down your powerful questions to use again later. You have to step into the unknown and live in the contextual moment. It can feel uncomfortable, but the results are well worth it.

Powerful questions framework

Here's a framework, a set of steps you can use to help you ask powerful questions more frequently.

**SEE-HEAR-SPEAK: A POWERFUL
QUESTIONS FRAMEWORK**

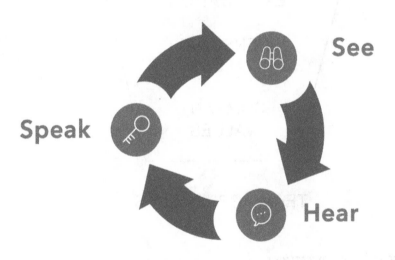

CHAPTER 6: ESTABLISH OPEN, HONEST, AND DIRECT COMMUNICATION

Step 1: Draft your rules of the game

Begin by creating three lists: a list of your expectations, a list of your personal values, and a list of values from other organizations you admire. As we begin the process, I encourage you to write down as much as possible in the early part of this brainstorm. What we are doing is gathering all of our ideas, without judging them as good and bad. Once we have all our ideas captured, we'll narrow down the ideas into a few core team agreements.

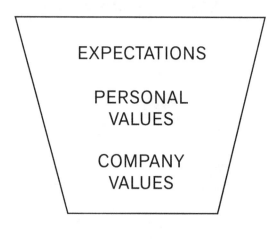

TEAM AGREEMENTS

List 1: Your expectations

Start by creating a list of all the expectations you have of your direct reports. To help you come up with your list, write down two or more bullets for each question below.

1. How do you know this person is a rock star on your team?

Examples

- He tells me when he's behind on a deliverable before the deadline has passed.

- She asks for help when she needs it.
- He is unafraid to challenge ideas of others, including me.
- She takes risks and is willing to make mistakes.

2. How do you know they're not a fit for your team?

Examples

- He thinks he knows all the answers.
- She makes the same mistakes over and over again.
- She doesn't set deadlines for her deliverables.
- He blames others for his mistakes.

3. What is one thing people on your team do (or one person does) that pisses you off?

Examples

- Show up late to meetings.
- Don't have an agenda prepared for a meeting.
- Don't do what they say they will do.
- Need to be told the same thing ten times to make one change.

**4. What expectations do you have that you haven't shared
with your team?**

Examples

- Before you say something won't work, do the work and test
your assumptions.

- Assume everyone on our team is working together to get to
the best possible outcome; no one is trying to intentionally
harm you.

- Don't just identify problems; come to me with a plan to
solve the problem, even if it's as simple as brainstorming a
solution together.

List 2: Your personal values

ACTIVITY: FIVE WORDS TO DESCRIBE YOU

At the top of a piece of paper, write down the words "I am . . ."
Close your eyes, then put your left hand on your stomach and
your right hand on your heart, feeling it beating, pumping
blood to all the vital organs in your body. Take a deep breath
in, slowly inhaling for five seconds, holding for one and releasing for five. Repeat this for five breaths. After the fifth breath,
open your eyes and write down any words to describe yourself.
Don't think; just write the first words that come to your mind.

If you pause, you are likely thinking about the words to
describe yourself instead of letting them come from within,

from your core. If this happens, stop, even if you're only at one word.

Share your list with a close friend, a family member, and a coworker. Ask them to share their opinion on the accuracy of these words in describing you and whether they feel the urge to offer a word or two that were missed. You can choose to add their words to your list, or not. These words are yours. Here are mine as a thought starter for you.

I am. . .

- Loving
- Caring
- Funny
- Honest
- Courageous

List 3: Values you admire

Finally, make a list of values that your company currently holds and ones you like from other companies that aren't already on list 2. Look at other team agreements you've seen from brands you like, from competitors you admire, and from mentors you look up to. There are great team agreements all around us, so take a moment to write down your favorites now.

Drafting your team agreements

Now what we are going to do is narrow down our ideas from all the lists to come up with your team agreements.

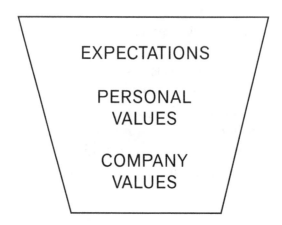

TEAM AGREEMENTS

Look back at your three lists and circle the five most important values and expectations. The question I want you to focus on when narrowing down your list to five, when deciding which expectation to keep and which value to let go of, is this: *What agreements or values are most important for my team to perform at its best?*

Defining success

For each agreement, ask yourself how you will know if an employee is exhibiting this agreement. What would success look like? What actions would he or she take? This last step is crucial: The more specific you are, the easier it will be for you to hold your employees accountable to the agreements.

Step 2: Turn your agreements into action

After you've clearly defined your team agreements, the next step is to gain alignment with your team.

Here are a few steps to getting aligned:

- Schedule two meetings.

- Whiteboard your drafted agreements.

- Share the meaning of each agreement.

- Encourage your team to ask clarifying questions.

- Follow up in writing.

- Make deals as a team.

Step 3: Embed your agreements into your day-to-day work

After you have alignment on your agreements, you can start to make them a part of everyday life within your organization or team.

Here are some best practices for incorporating your agreements into your everyday people practices:

- Add your agreements to your interview process.

- Don't just assess performance KPI; add in values KPI too.

- Follow up and follow through.

Step 4: Model open, honest, and direct communication with your team

Team agreements are not meant to be used simply as inspirational quotes. To work, they need to be used daily.

Craig Wortmann, a clinical professor of innovation and entre-preneurship at Northwestern University's Kellogg School of

Management, teaches this four-step process for making feedback a habit with your team.

ACTIVITY: MAKE FEEDBACK A HABIT WITH YOUR TEAM

1. What's one thing you did that worked well?
2. Here's one thing I think you did that worked well . . .
3. What's one thing you would do differently?
4. Here's one thing I think you could do differently . . .

CHAPTER 7: HOLD CRITICAL CONVERSATIONS

What makes a conversation critical?

Here is a quick set of questions to ask in helping you determine if you need to have a critical conversation.

ACTIVITY: CRITICAL CONVERSATION CHECKLIST

☐ Is something at stake?

☐ What's the impact if nothing changes?

☐ Is action needed from both parties?

☐ Is it a conversation or ultimatum?

The steps of having a critical conversation

Part 1: Take a Step Back

STEP 1: IDENTIFY THE PURPOSE

ACTIVITY: IDENTIFY THE PURPOSE

- Document the purpose of the conversation you need to have.
- What are you hoping will be different as a result of having the conversation?

STEP 2: FOCUS ON THE FACTS

ACTIVITY: FOCUS ON THE FACTS

- Document the facts of your situation—and only the facts.
- What would the hidden camera see or hear?

STEP 3: OWN YOUR REACTIONS

ACTIVITY: OWN YOUR REACTIONS

- Go back to your situation, replay the inciting incident in your mind, and notice how it felt.
- What thought(s) crossed your mind?
- What emotions came over you?
- How did it feel in your body? Did the muscles in your neck tense, or was it a pain in your stomach?

STEP 4: STAND BY YOUR COMMITMENT

ACTIVITY: STAND BY YOUR COMMITMENT

- What is your commitment as a leader?
- Are you upholding that commitment in this conversation?

Part 2: Have the conversation

STEP 5: GIVE A HEADS-UP

STEP 6: SHARE WHAT DIDN'T WORK AND ITS IMPACT ON YOU

ACTIVITY: THE ROOT CAUSE

- Restate the purpose of the conversation.
- Write down what didn't work.
  - Look back at your facts section, and pick the action the other person did that didn't work. It is OK to share a few actions that highlight the main action.
  - For example, "Kevin left the room" highlights the main action of him shutting down the conversation after I shared a different idea.
- Document the impact of the main action.

STEP 7: MAKE A REQUEST

ACTIVITY: YOUR REQUEST

- Write down your request now.

STEP 8: CREATE AN OPENING FOR POSSIBILITY

ACTIVITY: DIAGRAMMING THE DISCUSSION

This diagram should give you a better picture of how important creating an opening is.

5 minutes Share what didn't work, its impact and your request

20 minutes Create an opening for possibility

5 minutes Align on next steps

STEP 9: ALIGN ON THE NEXT STEPS

SCRIPT FOR HOLDING A CRITICAL CONVERSATION

STEP 1: IDENTIFY THE PURPOSE

What are you hoping will be different as a result of having the conversation?

- I want us to be better at communicating disagreements with each other.

STEP 2: FOCUS ON THE FACTS

What would the hidden camera see or hear?

- Kevin raised his voice and asked me if I cared about the business and then left the room.

STEP 3: OWN YOUR REACTIONS

Go back to your situation, replay the inciting incident in your mind, and notice how it felt.

What thought crossed your mind?

- I thought he was being shortsighted and didn't respect or value my opinion.

What emotions came over you?

- Anger, fear, and doubt.

How did it feel in your body? Did the muscles in your neck tense, or was it a pain in your stomach?

- I clenched my fists and felt the muscles in my neck stiffen.

STEP 4: STAND IN YOUR COMMITMENT

What is your commitment as a leader? Are you upholding that commitment in this conversation?

- I want to help us unlock the potential of our business and thus of our working together.

STEP 5: GIVE A HEADS-UP

- "Kevin, I wanted to sit down because I'm concerned

continued

about how we communicate disagreements with each other. I'd like to share my perspective, hear yours, and have a conversation about how we can improve the way we communicate."

STEP 6: SHARE WHAT DIDN'T WORK AND ITS IMPACT ON YOU

- "During our account review meeting last week, after I shared an idea for how to solve ABC Corp.'s complaint, I noticed you ended the conversation by leaving the room."

- "It stopped our meeting in its tracks. We weren't able to come to a solution for how to approach ABC Corp. I fear our inability to communicate disagreements with each other will hold us back from serving our clients' needs and succeeding as a business."

STEP 7: MAKE A REQUEST

- "When we come to a disagreement, I'd like you to ask me for the reasoning behind my opinion."

STEP 8: CREATE AN OPENING FOR POSSIBILITY

- "I had to shut up and listen to Kevin's side of the story."

STEP 9: ALIGN ON THE NEXT STEPS

Get clear on your next steps in the meeting and follow up with an email.

Kevin, thank you for taking the time to sit down and talk about how we can improve the way we communicate with each other.

Here's what I heard as next steps from the conversation; please review and let me know if you heard the same. When we come to a disagreement, one that is heated, that ends up with us ending the meeting, this is what I understand:

- I agree to allow you space to think and remind myself that you are frustrated with the situation, not with me.

- You agree to come back to me within twenty-four hours to meet again and determine the best next steps together.

Is this what you heard too? If not, let's reconnect and realign on our actions.

Cheers,
Aaron

PUTTING IT ALL TOGETHER: STEPS TO MOVE FORWARD

The one-on-one meeting

Use this agenda outline as a launching point.

- **Updates:** Here is a chance for both of you to share any relevant updates, to review goals and actions taken from the last check-in.

- **Working items:** This is the time to help the employee with issues from the past week.

- **Action items:** End the meeting aligning on next steps for each of you; recapping this in an email is an effective way to hold both of you accountable.

The performance conversation

Make sure to hold a performance conversation—ideally quarterly or biannually.

Here are a few sample questions I ask my team:

- What are some significant accomplishments from last quarter?

- What didn't go as planned? What happened? What did you learn?

- What is an area of growth you want to focus on for next quarter?

- What can I do to better support you?

Plan for between sixty and ninety minutes for each review, with at least thirty minutes of prep time ahead of the meeting.

The self check-in

Here are three steps to follow when conducting your weekly self-reflection:

Reflect on the past week

Take a look at your calendar, your to-do list, and your goals to clarify what you accomplished, what you missed, what you did well, and what you're proud of. This step is designed to help you identify gaps and celebrate successes.

Plan the week ahead

Look at your calendar for next week. What do you have coming up? What prep work do you need to do? What big projects and small tasks do you need to accomplish by the end of the week? Use these questions to make your to-do list. If you don't have enough time to do everything on the list, look to the next paragraph.

Say no, delegate, or delay

Based on the meetings you already have on your calendar, your personal or family commitments, and the projects you need to make progress on in the coming week, you've likely planned more work than you have time to accomplish. Instead of telling yourself you can get it all done, be a bit more realistic and strategic. Use these four questions to determine what you are really going to get done in the week.

- What takes priority?
- What should you be saying no to?
- What can you delegate to someone else?
- What do you have to delay?

Once you've worked through these questions, you should have a more clearly defined plan of meetings, projects, and tasks. You're now set up for success in the next week.

Bonus Chapter

WHY MILLENNIALS ARE DIFFERENT

Intention: To share a different perspective on the millennial generation and the world of work.

R oughly once a week, I'm asked, "Are millennials really that different from other generations?" Yes and no. There is a confluence of factors that play into how the millennial generation is currently seen and understood. To help better explain what I mean, I'll share the pivotal factors that impact how we see millennials and the current world of work.

We are different generationally

Millennials, individuals born between 1982 and 1998, were raised with different inciting incidents (the 9/11 terrorist attacks), different economic factors (the 2008 market crash), and a different culture (helicopter parenting, car seats, and more), which helped to mold us as a population. Where baby boomers are loyal to their companies, and Generation X is more loyal to their careers, millennials' loyalties lie with their communities. We see work as a calling instead of as a job or even a career. Although it is subtle, this distinction does change the expectations we have for our jobs. Millennials show up looking to make an impact, to be a part of a team, and to do meaningful work that makes a difference in the world.

Millennials drive companies to challenge the status quo of how the workplace currently operates. To get the most of your people, you have to accept that challenge.

BOOMER	GEN X	MILLENNIAL
· Born 1946-1964	· Born 1965-1981	· Born 1982-1998
· Work is a career	· Work is a job	· Work is a calling
· Loyal to company	· Loyal to self	· Loyal to community
· Value experience	· Value productivity	· Value contribution
· Principled, resolute, creative	· Savy, practical, independent	· Selfless, rational, competent

A new model for the world of work

Over the past forty years, as technology has enabled us to automate basic tasks, the type of work we've done has changed. We are no longer on the assembly line, making the same widget repeatedly. We've moved from the working economy brought about by the Industrial

Revolution, to the knowledge economy, where companies ask their employees to come up with creative solutions to complex problems. It is no longer sufficient to simply know the task we need to have completed. As knowledge workers, we also need to see the bigger picture, the purpose of our work, and the problem it is solving for our clients to reach the most effective solution.

The old model, which is contradictory to the type of work we are asking people to do now, is being questioned by millennials. They are the first full generation to enter the workforce unbiased by the old working economy. Although the new type of work is completely different, the workplace model has yet to change. We are no longer working on assembly lines in factories; nevertheless, we are still expecting people to clock in to a physical office nine a.m. to five p.m. every weekday. Many companies are working off a broken model, where you are measured on the time you put in rather than the work you produce. Millennials, the gig economy, and the future of work are calling for companies to focus on outcomes, not hours.

The rise of on-demand

Millennials have grown up in an on-demand society with pretty much everything at our fingertips. Take a typical day in the life of a millennial, Chelsea.

Chelsea wakes up, realizes she's run out of milk, eggs, and mouthwash, so she hops onto Amazon. By the time she's home from the gym, there's a delivery at her doorstep. As she's finishing breakfast, she orders a ride to work. While at work, Chelsea toggles among her work email, chat, text messages, and social media. On her ride home, she orders dinner from her phone and gets it just in time to sit on her couch and choose among thousands of titles to binge watch for the night.

We live in a world where virtually anything can be taken care of in a matter of minutes, right from a device the size of our palm. The impact of our habits on society is noticeable. Our need for instant gratification is at an all-time high. If we want something, we no longer understand what it means to wait. This is not just a millennial thing; the need for instant gratification extends to all of us. The use of these new technologies is not limited to millennials. Rather, smartphones and all the rest have been adopted by nearly all generations. Even my seventy-six-year-old uncle walks into dinner with his Bluetooth earpiece in, placing orders on Amazon while at dinner from his smartphone. No matter the generation, we're no longer used to waiting for what we want because we've been so conditioned to not having to wait.

This omnipresence of social media combined with the on-demand lifestyle we live creates an urgency to take action, to leave where you are and find a new job now. The problem is, our social network is not an authentic place to connect with friends; instead, it's become a place to promote the best versions of ourselves—true or not—to the world. It's now easier than ever to see what everyone in our social network is doing, where your friend just traveled for vacation, which friend just got a new job, which one just quit their job and went off on a three-month road trip, who's been promoted, and whose company just raised a bunch of money. In this world, the grass is always greener someplace else; it makes you examine your life and how it compares to the photoshopped versions your network promotes on their feeds.

Our increased need for instant gratification, coupled with increased options and visibility of others' success, drives millennials to seek success, contribution, and personal growth at a more rapid rate than previous generations. Technology has accelerated the millennial timeline.

Acceleration of the midlife crisis

Rob, like many teenagers, went to high school with the goal, determined by his family, his teachers, and our society, of going to a good college. After college, the societal expectation is for Rob to get a good job. In order not to disrupt the status quo and mostly because he has adopted these expectations as his own, Rob found a good job.

Each day Rob woke up, went to work, did his job, then came home. This repeated for twenty years when one day Rob woke up asking himself, *What am I doing? Why am I here on this earth? What impact do I want to have on the world? What is my purpose?*

Rob hit his midlife crisis, a point in his life where he reexamines his goals and ambitions because for the very first time in his life, there is no one else to tell him what those goals should be. Now he's got to figure them out on his own.

Due to a changing world of work, an increased need for instant gratification, and a generation predisposed to seek purpose, millennials are starting to ask these same questions two to three years into their working lives. The midlife crisis has been moved up by fifteen to twenty years and has become, instead, a quarter-life crisis. We are asking at a younger age what we want for ourselves and our lives; what is our purpose?

Questions like these are leading to a generation of people with a stronger emphasis on finding meaningful work, connecting with others, and personal growth.

WHAT'S THE POINT?

Millennials expect more from their work; they want to know the work they are doing is making an impact. They want to feel connected to their team, company, and boss, and they want to continuously grow. To me, that's an admirable and empowered vision of the world, one where we are forced to think about work in a different light.

It's not only that millennials are a different generation. The world of work is changing, and as business owners, we must take notice and adapt or get left behind. For the companies and leaders who prefer to stick to the status quo, it can feel as if they are in a war against the millennial ideals. For businesses who are agile and forward thinking, this new millennial perspective can be their competitive advantage in this war for top talent.

ACKNOWLEDGMENTS

This book would not be possible without energy, passion, and support of my incredible wife and partner, Kim. She was the first set of eyes to review so much of this book. Thank you for giving me the critical feedback I needed to make this work. Thank you for believing in me and us.

Thank you to my team at Raise The Bar. You rock! To Tina for constantly finding new strategies to share our message and thought leadership with our community of leaders. To Caro for helping put this all together, for your brilliant ideas, your challenging questions, and your energy. To George, your wisdom and boldness make me a better coach and leader. To Shiri for working through these models and theories with our clients and me as we refined them and made them better with each round.

Thank you to everyone who's helped me become a better leader and person. To my first boss, Will, for giving me a shot, for thinking big, and allowing me the space to make mistakes and grow. To Marc, for forcing me to think differently, for challenging me while still showing you cared about me. To Andrew, for making me uncomfortable pretty much every day we worked together—I learned so many valuable lessons in such a short time.

Thank you to my entire family for consistently being there for me, for supporting and showing up the ways I needed. To my brother Ari, for pushing me to be better, for being the entrepreneur I can learn from, and for continuing to serve as an advisor and friend. To my brother Adam, thank you for always being there to hear my wins, my failures, and my dreams for Raise The Bar. For pushing me to get this book out into the world and for continually sharing positive encouragement when I needed it most.

NOTES

In this section, you'll find the sources used in this book along with links and notes for further reading.

INTRODUCTION

1. Joseph Luciani, "Why 80 Percent of New Year's Resolutions Fail," *US News & World Report*, accessed April 2019, https://health.usnews.com/health-news/blogs/eat-run/articles/2015-12-29/why-80-percent-of-new-years-resolutions-fail.

2. "The 2016 Deloitte Millennial Survey," Deloitte Global, accessed January 2017, https://www2.deloitte.com/content/dam/Deloitte/global/Documents/About-Deloitte/gx-millenial-survey-2016-exec-summary.pdf.

3. "The Deloitte Millennial Survey 2018," Deloitte Global, March 2018, www2.deloitte.com/global/en/pages/about-deloitte/articles/millennialsurvey.html; "How Millennials Want to Work and Live," Gallup, accessed December 2016, news.gallup.com/reports/189830/e.aspx.

4. Brandon Rigoni and Bailey Nelson, "For Millennials, Is Job-Hopping Inevitable?" Gallup, accessed November 2016, https://news.gallup.com/businessjournal/197234/millennials-job-hopping-inevitable.aspx?g_source=MILLENNIALS&g_medium=topic&g_campaign=tiles.

5. Natalie Kitroeff, "Unemployment Rate Hits 3.9%, a Rare Low, as Job

Market Becomes More Competitive," *The New York Times*, May 2018, https://www.nytimes.com/2018/05/04/business/economy/jobs-report. html; "The Employment Situation – March 2019," US Department of Labor, April 2019, https://www.bls.gov/news.release/pdf/empsit.pdf.

6. E. L. Deci & R. M. Ryan, *Intrinsic Motivation and Self-Determination in Human Behavior* (New York, NY: Plenum, 1985); E. L. Deci & R. M. Ryan, "The 'What' and 'Why' of Goal Pursuits: Human Needs and the Self-Determination of Behavior," *Psychological Inquiry* 11 (2000), 227–268; R. M. Ryan & E. L. Deci, "Self-determination Theory and the Facilitation of Intrinsic Motivation, Social Development, and Well-Being," *American Psychologist* 55 (2000), 68–78.

7. Tom Nolan, "The No. 1 Employee Benefit That No One's Talking About," Gallup, accessed November 2018, https://www.gallup.com/ workplace/232955/no-employee-benefit-no-one-talking.aspx.

CHAPTER 2

1. Larry Emond, "2 Reasons Why Employee Engagement Programs Fall Short," Gallup, accessed August 2017, www.gallup.com/ workplace/236147/reasons-why-employee-engagement-programs-fall-short.aspx?g_source=ALL_GALLUP_HEADLINES&g.

CHAPTER 3

1. Pierre Gurdjian, Thomas Halbeisen, and Kevin Lane, "Why Leadership-Development Programs Fail," McKinsey & Company, accessed March 2017, https://www.mckinsey.com/global-themes/leadership/why-leadership-development-programs-fail.

CHAPTER 4

1. "Some Interesting Facts about Listening," Transform Inc., accessed March 2017, https://transforminc.com/2014/07/interesting-facts-listening/.

2. Adam Grant, *Give and Take: Why Helping Others Drives Our Success* (New York: Penguin Books, 2013); R. Rosenthal and L. Jacobson, "Teachers' expectancies: Determinants of pupils' IQ gains," *Psychological Reports* 19 (1966): 115–118.

3. R. Rosenthal and L. Jacobson, *Pygmalion in the Classroom: Teacher Expectation and Pupils' Intellectual Development* (Bancyfelin, Carmarthen, Wales: Crown House Publishing, 1992).

4. Brené Brown, "RSA Short: Empathy," accessed January 2016, https://brenebrown.com/videos/rsa-short-empathy/.

CHAPTER 5

1. Amos Tversky and Daniel Kahneman, "Judgment under Uncertainty: Heuristics and Biases" (PDF), *Science* 185, no. 4157 (1974): 1124–1131, doi:10.1126/science.185.4157.1124, PMID 17835457 reprinted in Daniel Kahneman, Paul Slovic, Amos Tversky, eds., *Judgment Under Uncertainty: Heuristics and Biases* (Cambridge, UK: Cambridge University Press, 1982): 3–20, ISBN 9780521284141. See also: Michael Lewis, *The Undoing Project: A Friendship That Changed Our Minds* (New York: W. W. Norton & Company, 2016) and Daniel Kahneman, *Thinking, Fast and Slow* (New York: Farrar, Straus and Giroux, 2011).

2. Steven Ruiz, "Re-scouting Tom Brady at Michigan: Why NFL teams had no excuse for passing on him," For The Win, accessed January 2019, https://ftw.usatoday.com/2017/10/nfl-patriots-tom-brady-draft-college-michigan-scouting-report.

3. Drake Baer, "Kahneman: Your Cognitive Biases Act Like Optical Illusions," The Cut, accessed December 2017, https://www.thecut.com/2017/01/kahneman-biases-act-like-optical-illusions.html.

4. Amos Tversky and Daniel Kahneman, "Extensional Versus Intuitive Reasoning: The Conjunction Fallacy in Probability Judgment," *Psychological Review*, 90:4 (1983): 293-315.

5. Gino Wickman, *Traction: Get a Grip on Your Business* (Dallas, TX: BenBella Books, 2007).

6. I drew inspiration for this framework from the ancient Japanese proverb on the three wise monkeys and the insights of my colleague George. "Three Wise Monkeys," Wikipedia, accessed March 2019, https://en.wikipedia.org/wiki/Three_wise_monkeys#Meaning_of_the_proverb.

CHAPTER 6

1. Charles Duhigg, "What Google Learned From Its Quest to Build the Perfect Team," *The New York Times*, February 25, 2016, https://www.nytimes.com/2016/02/28/magazine/what-google-learned-from-its-quest-to-build-the-perfect-team.html; "Understand Team Effectiveness," re:Work, accessed April 2018, https://rework.withgoogle.com/print/guides/5721312655835136/.

2. Amy C. Edmondson, "Managing the Risk of Learning: Psychological Safety in Work Teams," Harvard Business School Working Paper, No. 02-062, March 2002; Adam Grant, "The Daily Show's Secret to Creativity," WorkLife with Adam Grant, TED.com, March 8, 2018, https://www.ted.com/talks/worklife_with_adam_grant_creative_burstiness_at_the_daily_show.

3. Adam Grant, "Why You Should Stop Serving the Feedback Sandwich," Inc.com, accessed February 2019, https://www.inc.com/linkedin/adam-grant/stop-serving-feedback-sandwich-adam-grant.html.

4. Craig Wortmann, "Performance Feedback: 4-Step Model to Give & Receive," LinkedIn, accessed April 2017, www.linkedin.com/pulse/performance-feedback-4-step-model-give-receive-craig-wortmann/.

CHAPTER 7

1. Marshall Rosenberg, *Nonviolent Communication: A Language of Life* (Encinitas, CA: PuddleDancer Press, 2003).

2. Viktor E. Frankl, *Man's Search for Meaning* (1946). Reprint edition (Boston: Beacon Press, 2006).

3. Michelle Norris and Melissa Block, "Civil-Rights Activist, Ex-Klansman C. P. Ellis," *All Things Considered*, National Public Radio, November 8, 2005, www.npr.org/templates/story/story.php?storyId=4994854. Diane Bloom, "An Unlikely Friendship," PBS, February 1, 2019, https://www.pbs.org/video/an-unlikely-friendship-tbnri0/.

CHAPTER 8

1. E. Aronson, B. Willerman, & J. Floyd, (1966). "The effect of a pratfall on increasing interpersonal attractiveness," *Psychonomic Science* 4, no. 6 (1966), 227–228.

ABOUT THE AUTHOR

Open, Honest, and Direct: A Guide to Unlocking Your Team's Potential is Aaron Levy's first book. In addition to being a new author, Aaron is the Founder and CEO of Raise The Bar, an organization focused on helping companies create high-performing teams by building better leaders.

Aaron is the host of the *Open, Honest, and Direct* podcast, the co-director of Startup Grind Chicago, a Thrive Global contributor, an 1871 mentor, an ICF Certified Coach, and a member of the Forbes Coaches Council.

Over the last decade, Aaron has worked with over 7,500 business leaders in a variety of industries, inspiring them to define their goals, create tactical action plans, and achieve sustained success. Aaron is on a mission to transform the manager role by empowering each manager with the tools, skills, and training to be leaders of people who unlock the potential of their team.

To learn more about Aaron, visit www.raisebar.co and www.openhonestanddirect.com.

CPSIA information can be obtained
at www.ICGtesting.com
Printed in the USA
BVHW031036310521
608469BV00018B/713

9 781632 992376